Olena Berezovska

ANGEL

International Academy of Healthy Life

2025

Angel

© 2024-2025 by Olena Berezovska
228 pages
Published by:
International Academy of Healthy Life
Mississauga, Ontario

Author:
Olena Berezovska

ISBN: 978-0-9867786-8-1

Angel is a journey of hope, resilience, and the profound connection between human souls. Olena Berezovska weaves a narrative that delves into the intricacies of human emotions, exploring themes of healing, redemption, and the unseen forces that guide us through life's most challenging moments. This book invites readers to reflect on the strength within and the beauty of compassion in unexpected places.

Cover Design:
Olena Berezovska

Printed in Canada

Dear readers,

It is with great joy that I introduce my book, 'Angel.' This work, born from my personal journey, is a testament to the light and warmth that spirituality can bring to our souls. Some of you, who know me primarily as a scientist and physician, may find it surprising that I've ventured into such a subject. For those who are new to my work, this book offers a unique opportunity to delve into my life and experiences on a deeper level.

So, why "Angel"? Why a spiritual work that resonates with my soul and, hopefully, touches yours, even if not everyone's? Why not another scientific treatise filled with facts and research? Or a collection of humorous stories and poems? The answer lies in the contradictions within my life, just as in yours. There are experiences, events, and truths that demand to be expressed, no matter how complex or personal they may be.

Reflecting on these moments and sorting through my thoughts, I realized that keeping these insights locked inside was no longer an option. Some of what I share may seem unusual, mystical, or even unscientific. Yet here I am, offering you my soul, open and vulnerable, along with everything I've experienced. It's a leap of faith, a trust in you, my readers, to understand and accept me.

At the same time, I cannot erase these events from my life or pretend they never happened. Nor can I create a more "acceptable" version of myself just to fit into someone else's idea of normalcy. These experiences are part of who I am. And I know, with complete certainty, that I am not alone in this. Many of you will understand and support me.

Many of you believe in God, prophets, and saints or follow religions and spiritual traditions. This is a natural part of human life. For me, "Angel" is just as natural, a small yet meaningful piece of my life, and it deserves to exist exactly as I share it with you. My knowledge and life experience can benefit many, and the positive emotions and feelings I offer bring balance and renewed confidence to those in need.

As I penned this book, my heart was light, my face adorned with a smile, and my soul at peace. I hope that as you embark on this journey through its pages, you find not just joy and relief, but also faith and hope, love and light. May this book serve as a source of solace and inspiration, guiding you toward a renewed sense of purpose and confidence.

Thank you from the bottom of my heart for not passing this book by. Your interest and support mean the world to me. I wish you a meaningful and uplifting journey alongside me and the Angel.

With love, Olena Berezovska

Acknowledgments

Every creative endeavor demands time and resources, often significant ones, and inevitably, our lives revolve around the creation process. This journey, in turn, impacts the lives of those around us, especially our closest family and friends. For that reason, I want to express my deepest gratitude to my family, my husband Yuriy, and my children, Yulia and Alex, for their patience and understanding during the times when "mom was glued to the computer, and it was best to leave her undisturbed."

A special thanks goes to Olena Kostyukova, the visionary founder and leader of the medical network Likar.Info. Thanks to her, my book "Thousands of Questions and Answers on Gynecology" came to life, along with other medical and health-related projects that are now in the works. Olena was also the very first reader of "Angel," even before it was complete. Her encouraging words, "I've been longing for a book like this! Keep writing!" motivated me to see this project through to the end.

I am also incredibly grateful to Roman Shevtsiv, an old friend, classmate, colleague, and talented, compassionate physician. His unwavering support and dedicated efforts helped bring this book to life.

Of course, my heartfelt thanks go to you, dear readers, for choosing this book, investing your time in reading it, and reaching the final page. Your interest and support mean the world to me.

And naturally, I must thank the Angel, whose presence and influence have been felt throughout this journey.

I'd love to hear from you if you have any feedback, suggestions, or thoughts. Your engagement with this book is greatly appreciated.

Finally, we met again. He sat alone on a bench in a vast park, smiling. Was he smiling at himself or the World around him? I couldn't tell. The gentle melody of birdsong filled the air, and a soft breeze stirred the leaves. He radiated a deep, serene peace, leaving me feeling tranquil.

"Why here, of all places?" I asked.

"Wasn't it you who imagined this place?" the Angel asked quietly.

"That's true," I admitted. "But does that mean all of this, and you, are just figments of my imagination?"

The Angel smiled softly. After a brief pause, he replied:

"Are you sure that reality itself isn't filtered through imagination?"

"Every person experiences their version of reality," I answered, feeling like a student eager to impress her Teacher. "It's a reality shaped by how we perceive the world, through the lens of our self, both body and consciousness."

"Then it's possible," the Angel continued, "that what some consider to be reality may be nothing more than imagination, and the opposite might also be true."

"We'll talk about that another time," I said.

I sat down beside Him without really knowing why. It wasn't a decision; it felt natural, like I belonged there, sitting quietly beside the Angel.

"Do you have a name?" I asked Him.

"I do," the Angel replied calmly.

"And are you an angel?" I continued with a hint of doubt in my voice.

"You don't truly doubt it. So why ask?"

"Because, for many people, angels are nothing more than imaginary beings from some otherworldly realm," I said.

A warm, radiant smile spread across the Angel's face.

"My dear, there is no 'otherworld.' There is only the World. The Universe and more beyond it. All of it is whole and interconnected," the Angel explained gently.

"I understand," I murmured.

"And so, we return to the imagination. If someone imagines me as a winged, genderless being, that is what they wish to see in their mind and their reality."

7

"But I didn't expect to see you as a man," I objected.

"It's easier for you to see me this way. Opposites naturally attract. If I had appeared as a woman, you would have called me a fairy, a sorceress, or..."

"Or Baba Yaga!" I burst out, laughing before He could finish.

"Do I look that frightening?" the Angel asked with playful concern. "Ah, yes, it must be the black."

"Why black?" I asked, curious now.

"Less dirt sticks to it," He replied with a sly smile, then burst into laughter. "I'm just teasing. Black absorbs everything while reflecting nothing. But we can appear in any form, wearing anything."

"With wings or without?" I asked.

"Either way. Wings, if you prefer."

"And yet... what's your name, Angel?"

"Just call me Angel because I am not alone; there are many of us," he said gently. As for my name, it doesn't matter right now. Someday, if you need to, you'll know it."

Being with Him felt so right, calm, and peaceful. I didn't want to go anywhere or say anything, yet my mind buzzed with a flurry of new thoughts.

***

I recalled our first meeting... But why do I call it the "first"? It likely wasn't. I must have forgotten many others. My mind, overwhelmed by an endless stream of information, most unnecessary, had become a vast, cluttered warehouse, with some shelves buried in the dust of time. Occasionally, fleeting images from past lives flash before my eyes, though many of them are lost to memory. Yet, one thing I've never forgotten is the moment of my fortunate non-return — the time I almost didn't return from the place I came from before entering this earthly world.

Yes, fortunate non-return is the right way to describe it. When I tried to go back there, I was sent back because there were important reasons for staying. And thank God I returned. It wasn't my time yet. The relief and gratitude I felt upon realizing this were overwhelming, a reassurance that there's still more to experience in this earthly life.

To be precise, I chose to return, though, for a long time, I thought otherwise, believing I hadn't wanted to return. But I was wrong. A powerful bond connected me with many people in my earthly life, a bond so deep that it wouldn't allow me to remain in that other realm. It was this profound connection, this web of relationships, that pulled me back, making me realize the power and importance of human connections.

God never forces us to return against our will nor compels us to leave if we genuinely wish to stay. Such are Their laws, a profound understanding of which can enlighten us and guide us in our journey through life.

***

It was a simple, routine operation, yet it left a profound imprint on me, turning my life upside down. The anesthesiologist, stifling a lazy yawn, administered the anesthesia. I was convinced I wouldn't fall asleep. But then, my eyelids grew heavy, and before me stretched an infinite expanse of emptiness, not emptiness, but a vast, black void.

I found myself drifting through this space, which slowly began to fill with billions of shimmering stars. Then, a tunnel appeared, its far end illuminated by a brilliant light, not blinding but irresistibly warm, drawing me closer with its comforting embrace. The deeper I ventured, the more everything felt right, as if peace itself was welcoming me.

I became aware of two beings accompanying me, flying beside me. They exuded kindness, their forms composed of some unknown, plasma-like essence, both strange and yet strangely reassuring.

Then, I was enveloped in a state of pure, boundless Bliss. It was unlike anything I could ever describe — no language, no words in the world could capture it. It was a profound feeling that once experienced, it became impossible to forget.

Suddenly, a sharp turn to the left led me through an unexpected doorway in the tunnel. Though calling it a "door" doesn't quite fit, it doesn't matter now: I found myself in a room with no visible windows or doors. And I wasn't just me anymore. I could see myself from the outside, suspended as if lying on an operating table, though no table was there. I saw everything around me with perfect clarity.

Four humanoid figures stood near me — two by my arms, two by my legs. They weren't human, though they had human-like forms, their gender indiscernible. Their silver suits emitted a soft, diffused glow, blending seamlessly with the soothing white Light radiating from the walls.

What remains etched in my memory are their Eyes and Smiles. They radiated pure kindness, genuine warmth, and love, shimmering with compassion.

And then, silence.

"What is all this?" I thought. "Why have I been stopped? Who are we waiting for?"

Only silence greeted me, broken only by the warmth in their gaze.

"How long must we wait?" I wondered again.

Then, a Voice, calm, kind, and neither male nor female, spoke directly into the core of my awareness:

"Let her go. It's not time yet."

I felt my body shift, drawn back toward the tunnel, descending slowly...

"Nooo!" I kept screaming, pulling farther away from the Bliss, the peace slipping beyond my grasp.

When I opened my eyes, the sterile and bright ceiling of the operating room swam into view. Around me, the doctors moved busily; the procedure was already finished.

"Wake up! It's all done!" someone chirped.

"Do you know where I've been?" I croaked, my voice rough and dry.

A few chuckles rippled through the room.

"I was on my way There," I said with conviction, though my tongue felt thick in my parched mouth.

More amused chuckles followed.

"Yeah, everyone flies off somewhere," the anesthesiologist quipped with a grin.

I shifted my gaze to a doctor standing nearby, and his thoughts appeared as clearly as if they were written before me.

"You'll make it to lunch, don't worry," I said with a small smile, knowing that food was the only thing on his mind.

Beside me, a young intern stood quietly, holding my hand. I'd known her for years. She enjoyed being near me, though I had never considered her a friend. Something was always missing — that deeper connection that true friendship requires.

I looked at her now, and her thoughts unfolded as clearly as spoken words.

I tried to keep my mouth shut, but at that moment, my conscious and subconscious minds were entirely out of sync.

"Why are you always jealous of me?" I blurted, unable to stop the words. "Look at me! I'm lying here, weak, useless, and forgotten. I've lost my child. And you? You've always had more than I ever did, more than enough. What more could you possibly want?" My tongue moved freely, without any control.

The nearby nurse glanced at the young doctor and said dismissively, "Don't mind her. People say all sorts of nonsense after anesthesia and surgery. She'll be back to normal soon."

Am I not normal? Or am I not their version of normal?

They transferred me to a hospital room. As I lay on the gurney, wheeled down the corridor, I caught sight of the old professor at the far end. I was supposed to take a critical exam tomorrow. Still, I only wanted to close my eyes, feel Bliss, and see that Light again. "Why? Why? Why?" I kept asking, though the question wasn't directed at myself but at Them, those who remained beyond this world I had been forced to return to. "I don't want to be here! I don't want to come back!"

Too late, my dear...

The old professor rushed toward me when he spotted me on the gurney. He entered the room just as the nurses were helping me into bed. I lay there, half-conscious, frustration and disappointment weighing heavily on me.

"What happened?" the professor asked the nurse standing beside me. "I hope it's not an ectopic pregnancy."

For some reason, the thought came to him that I, his student, must have fainted during a procedure due to a suspected ectopic pregnancy. It was the first diagnosis that would naturally cross a gynecologist's mind upon seeing a woman in such a dazed, semi-conscious state.

"Didn't anyone teach you to knock?" I snapped, my voice was sharper than I intended.

Immediately, regret flooded my mind. "Dear God, that's not what I wanted to say. How could I speak like that to my old professor?" But the words had already escaped, and my tongue kept moving.

"Leave me alone! Just leave me alone — everyone!"

I squeezed my eyes shut, desperate to disconnect, drift off, or at least escape into oblivion — anything to see that Light again and feel that Bliss. But instead, I tumbled into a vast, black void where there was nothing to see or hear — only silence.

For a long time, I struggled with the burden of returning to this world, constantly replaying the experience of my journey into another dimension. The memories of that otherworldly flight lingered, haunting me. It took time, but eventually, I began to understand why I had been sent back.

One day, as I watched my two little ones playing, I realized that I couldn't leave them. They needed my love, my care, my warmth. How could I have wished to leave this world where my children deeply needed me? How could I have longed for some distant, otherworldly bliss when the truest Bliss was before me, the sparkling laughter of my joyful children?

Paradise isn't somewhere far away, beyond this life. It is here, in the moments we live and cherish, in the love we give and receive, and in the joy we find when we fully embrace every moment of our lives.

***

I rushed into the large room, where the only light came from the flickering flames in the fireplace.

It was a quiet winter evening. The Angel lay comfortably on a soft leather sofa, a book resting in his hands.

"Sorry I'm late," I said, settling onto the plush rug by the fire.

The Angel looked at me with a gentle smile. "How can you be late to your own home? Besides, there's no such thing as 'late.'"

"Really?" I asked, intrigued. "Then what is there?"

"Everything unfolds in its own time," the Angel replied, his words carrying the weight of quiet wisdom.

"And time is relative..." I murmured, trailing off in thought.

The patient and serene Angel seemed to wait, allowing me space to explore my reflections.

"Because people create obstacles and limitations for themselves," he said finally. "They dramatize their experiences, making events seem more final than they are."

"I would, but it's too late to change anything now," I mused aloud. "I hear that all the time."

"That's just an illusion," the Angel explained. "As long as one hasn't built a mental barrier, shutting themselves off from possibility, 'too late' does not exist. Time limits only appear when the mind invents them."

"Exactly. It's just a word we use to mask our dishonesty — toward others, but never ourselves," I added.

The Angel smiled. "You're both a good student and a good teacher. So, tell me, what do you mean by dishonesty? Toward others or oneself?"

"No one deceives themselves," I said. "Deep down, *people always know what they do or do not want*. 'I want' cannot be conditional. But out of fear — of seeming selfish, unkind, or irresponsible—people claim they would like to do something, all while constructing excuses: time constraints, external obligations, self-imposed barriers."

"Have you considered," the Angel asked, "that many people want and fear something simultaneously? That contradiction creates an inner conflict, making it difficult to choose, even to admit the struggle to oneself."

"In the end, people usually follow whatever aligns with their strongest impulse. Rarely does anyone choose against their true desires, no matter how selfish or what it may cost."

The Angel listened intently, nodding.

How often do we confine ourselves within imaginary boundaries — rigid and sometimes utterly absurd?

It is never too late to open the door to someone we love, if that desire is genuine and not merely an empty sentiment. It is never too late to help someone in need — so long as the need is genuine and not an illusion of our own making.

But what about death? What about irreversible loss? In those moments, we say it is too late. Yet, is it? Or is it simply no longer the right time?

What feels like 'too late' to us may be perfectly timed from another perspective — one beyond our dimension of space and time.

"Why won't you tell me your name?" I asked the Angel, breaking the silence.

"A name is just a word people choose for various reasons. A name means 'one,' but as I've told you, I am not one. I don't have a physical form; everything you see merely manifests through your imagination."

"Or is it imagination taking form through materialization?" I asked curiously.

"Not quite," the Angel replied, his wisdom shining through. "Could you perceive Us in everything around you without needing the form in which you now see me?"

"It's hard to imagine holding a conversation with thin air," I said, laughing as the thought of talking to nothing and no one amused me for a moment. In some ways, many people may talk to themselves after all. But any conversation, at its core, requires at least two: one to speak and one to listen to."

"Every person's name carries a unique meaning," said the Angel.

"And what about the names of Angels and other non-human beings?" I asked.

"They carry no meaning. We communicate on the level of informational energy, where names are unnecessary. We have no names and never did. But explaining this to people is nearly impossible. They assign us ranks, titles, degrees, and positions — labels that mirror the structure of their human world."

"I know what my name means."

"Olena. It means 'Chosen.' But it holds many other meanings as well."

"Yes, it comes from Greek. For the longest time, I couldn't understand what or who I was chosen by," I said.

"And now? Do you understand?"

"Yes! I do. Chosen by Life, by You, by Myself. Just Chosen. But aren't all people chosen?" I asked the Angel.

"All people are chosen at birth, though most forget it," he replied. "For many, that sense of being chosen becomes irrelevant, replaced by imitating others they believe to be chosen."

"Chosen by whom? God or people?"

"By everything and everyone."

"Are you saying you choose even negative ideals?" I asked, my curiosity burning inside me.

"People themselves often create negative ideals because what is negative to you might be positive to someone else," the Angel answered. "You see only negativity, forgetting that every coin has many sides."

"Many, or just three?"

The Angel smiled and replied,

"Why don't you count?"

I cherish these moments, perhaps hours when I can be with the Angel, though, in truth, He or They are always nearby.

"I want to write a book about You," I said.

"Did you mean about us?" the Angel asked gently. "About all of us, including you."

"I want to share the knowledge I receive from You," I explained. "But so often, I just don't have time to write it down... and I struggle to remember it, too."

"You don't need to remember everything," the Angel reassured me, his patience a comforting presence. "You already know how and where to find this knowledge. And you know whom to ask any question, and you will always receive an answer. We respond to every question people ask; the problem is people don't always know how to listen. Much of what you seek is already written down. People call it 'human wisdom' or 'the wisdom of civilizations'."

It is that simple! We so often speak more than we listen. Our tongue takes over when we talk, and our ears merely catch our voice. To truly hear another person, you need only stop and listen. To hear what they tell you, you must first clear your mind and free it of your thoughts and the countless answers you've crafted before the question is even asked.

"This will be my favorite book," I said.

"That's not true," the Angel replied with a gentle smile, his understanding embracing me. "Every book you write will be your favorite. How could you not love your creations, just as a parent cannot divide their children into loved and unloved? Every work you create is like a child; you pour pieces of yourself: your emotions, soul, life, and even material value."

How swiftly time flies for me, though not for the Angel. How can I learn to soar through time, so it remains still while I move freely?

"It's simple. Look at everything from the perspective of time," the Angel said, quickly reading my thoughts.

"Alright, then. I'm off! Until we meet again beyond time and space!"

***

My first encounter with 'otherworldly beings' happened long before I fully understood the world, and it was anything but pleasant. These beings, which I later understood as a manifestation of my subconscious, played a significant role in my journey of resilience and survival.

Despite the daunting combination of pregnancy and a sudden, severe lung inflammation, I refused to succumb to the neglect of the hospital's doctors. Each day, my condition worsened, but I clung to hope, not just for my health but for the well-being of my unborn child. This resilience in the face of medical neglect is a testament to the human spirit's ability to endure.

I was offered various treatments, but no one conducted a thorough examination. I refused the new, potent antibiotics, fearing they might harm my tiny baby, whose gender I didn't yet know and whose survival was still uncertain, as I was only 16 weeks along. My first pregnancy had ended in severe illness following the loss of the fetus, making this pregnancy especially significant to me, both as a woman and as a hopeful mother.

I was deteriorating rapidly, not by the day but by the hour. Something was compressing my airways, and I was gasping for breath during terrifying bouts of suffocation. Although I lacked the classic symptoms of pneumonia, I could occasionally feel the fluid shifting in my lungs whenever I changed positions.

The doctors usually listened to my lungs while I was lying down, resting, which made it difficult for them to detect anything. All they could report was "muffled breathing." A chest puncture was performed to extract fluid or at least provide some answers, but the procedure was excruciating and ultimately futile, leaving the doctors even more perplexed than before.

One day, a young medical student sat beside me, asking about my medical history. I suggested she try listening to my lungs while I changed positions. What she heard left her stunned; it sounded like the roar of a rushing river. Alarmed, she ran to the doctor's office, trying to explain her discovery. But instead of taking her seriously, they laughed it off, dismissing her findings as insignificant. Meanwhile, my condition continued to deteriorate with no improvement in sight.

A month passed, and a doctor approached my grieving parents and husband. "It would be best to take her home," she said, "so she can... pass away in familiar surroundings." That was the verdict, not mine, but theirs. The doctors had grown tired of a stubborn patient who refused a toxic dose of experimental antibiotics and insisted on keeping the pregnancy.

I asked the doctors, "If I agree to the antibiotics, what are the chances my baby will survive unharmed?"

"There are no such chances," they replied, "because these antibiotics are strictly contraindicated during pregnancy. But we're not thinking about your baby right now; it's unlikely to survive. You need to survive. The best option is to terminate the pregnancy."

"But performing an abortion during an active infection isn't safe, is it?" I protested. "That means I could die from the anesthesia since I can barely breathe on my own or from the procedure itself, given how weak I am. On top of that, there's the risk of a systemic infection spreading through my bloodstream and lymphatic system. What are my chances of surviving the abortion?"

"Very low, considering your condition," the doctors admitted.

"So, I could die not only from the pneumonia and pleurisy but also from the abortion and the risk of infection spreading?"

"Exactly," they confirmed without hesitation.

"So, what's the point of ending my baby's life if both of us have the same chance of surviving or dying?" That was my final question.

Even when the doctors gave up on me, effectively sentencing me to death, I refused to accept their verdict. I stood my ground, denying the abortion they recommended, and in doing so, I reclaimed my agency and my right to fight for my life. My defiance in the face of such dire circumstances was a testament to the strength of the human spirit, inspiring others never to give up.

The room housed eight patients, all with lung-related illnesses. Two women showed unmistakable signs of active tuberculosis, something even I, as a fourth-year medical student, could easily recognize. Yet the doctors paid little attention to them.

Despite my dire situation, I couldn't ignore the suffering of my fellow patients. Two women, showing unmistakable signs of active tuberculosis, took care of me during my stay despite their impending fate. Their selflessness and compassion in the face of their suffering left a lasting impression on me, reminding me of the shared humanity that binds us all.

During the day, the ward was alive with activity, like a buzzing hive, filled with constant chatter among patients and visitors. But at night, it became a symphony of coughs, snores, and groans. I couldn't sleep at all, partly because of the suffocating fits and partly because of the relentless noise.

When I heard the doctors' "verdict," I couldn't sleep for hours. Half-sitting, I stared blankly at the walls, the ceiling, and the sleeping patients, my mind numb. All I wanted was to drift off, escape into sleep, and forget this room and its suffering inhabitants, if only for a little while. But the suffocating tightness in my chest wouldn't let me relax, let alone find peace.

Then, out of nowhere, I noticed a shadow in the corner, a black, ominous shadow.

At that time, I had been raised as an atheist, yet for some reason, the thought instantly came to me: "The Angel of Death." I glanced at the clock to ensure I wasn't dreaming — ten minutes to four in the morning. I pinched my arm, and the sting confirmed it: I was wide awake. But the shadow remained, unmoving as if waiting.

With no other option, I found myself drawn into a strange, silent exchange, a conversation not with words but with thoughts.

"I've come for you," the shadow whispered into my mind. Its face was hidden beneath the folds of a black robe, shrouding any hint of a body or head it might possess—if it even had such things. In truth, I can't say for sure whether it felt like *she* had come or *he* had come. All I knew was that something, someone had come for me. All I knew was that something had come for me.

Strangely, I felt no fear. Instead, an unshakable calm settled over me, a testament to my resilience in the face of the unknown. My ability to maintain composure in such a situation was a source of admiration for those around me.

"I am not ready to die," I declared firmly, projecting the thought outward.

The shadow remained silent.

"Listen," I continued, "there's a new life growing inside me, a child who must be born. That's why I have no right to die. Find someone else—someone weak, frail, whose time has already passed, someone who can no longer savor this world and leave me in peace. I cannot die. I won't."

The shadow lingered in silence, then vanished as if it had never existed.

I struggled to make sense of it all. I didn't want to believe it was real, that I wasn't dreaming, that it wasn't just the product of a mind exhausted by illness. And with those thoughts swirling in my head, I fell asleep.

My husband rushed into the room early in the morning, visibly shaken.

"We got some terrible news," he said, his voice heavy. "My nanny, Grandma Ksenia, has passed away. They're asking me to come for the funeral, but I can't leave you here alone."

His words sent a chill through me, but I forced myself to stay calm.

"When did she die? Do you know what time?" I asked softly.

"I'm not sure," Yuri answered. "Sometime early this morning."

"Go to the village," I said gently. "Say goodbye to her. Don't worry about me — I'll be fine now." Then, after a pause, I added, "Please, find out exactly what time Grandma Ksenia passed. It's important."

I couldn't bring myself to tell even my husband what had happened during the night. I didn't want him to misunderstand. We didn't discuss God, life after death, or angels back then. We were just young students, focused on school, with no time for such things.

Although my husband didn't want to leave, I insisted. While he was away, my father "happened" to cross paths with an old acquaintance, a man holding a significant position within the party leadership. During their conversation, my father mentioned my illness and the fact that I was being discharged home. Deeply moved by my situation, the man offered to transfer me to an exclusive hospital reserved for communist leaders and high-ranking officials, a place where only the most privileged received care, a hospital for the "chosen by the people."

My husband returned the next day. I asked him to tell me everything about the last days and final moments of his nanny's life.

When I first met her, Grandma Ksenia was already quite old. She lived with her niece in a small, impoverished hut, barely scraping by. We became friends quickly, and she often shared stories about my husband's childhood and memories of his sister, mother, and uncles, whom she had cared for as a nanny while also managing the household.

In the final year of her life, Grandma Ksenia suffered several strokes, leaving her paralyzed. She passed away around four in the morning, the same day the Angel of Death visited me.

I kept what happened that night to myself for a long time, doing my best to forget both the shadow and our conversation, the way one tries to forget dreams, fantasies, or nightmares. I didn't want to become the subject of ridicule among my loved ones, hear them mock me as "crazy," or tell me I needed "help."

People often become victims of those who lack the kindness to listen or the openness to accept someone else's truth because we carry our version. We hear only what we want to hear and see only what we want to see.

Did I want to see the Angel of Death, even though I didn't believe in angels or God? One thing I knew for sure: I didn't want to die. I wasn't ready. I wanted something to happen, something that would transform my life, not take it away. That something turned out to be the beginning of a new chapter. I opened the door to the WORLD, merging the material and immaterial into a single concept: the essence of LIFE in all its forms and manifestations.

I gave birth to a healthy, beautiful baby girl right on time, and from the very start, we shared a warm, open bond, a connection that has only grown stronger over the years.

A year and five months later, I gave birth to a son. The pregnancy was smooth, and the delivery was remarkably painless. Our baby boy was always smiling, never fussy, and filled our days with joy, bringing us immense happiness as we embraced parenthood wholeheartedly.

***

Many people confine themselves within artificial shells, shielding themselves from the outside world, particularly from information that challenges materialistic or physical explanations. However, the mysteries of the universe, the 'unusual' phenomena, are not to be feared but to be marveled at. They are awe-inspiring and can be explained by the laws we already know. But do we truly understand all the laws of the universe? Every science field has gaps that gradually fill over time, inviting us to explore and marvel at the unknown, sparking inspiration and curiosity.

As humanity evolves, so does life itself and science. Today's science stands far beyond the achievements of the last century, and the continuous evolution of science promises even more exciting discoveries in the future. The future of science is a beacon of hope, promising a world of new possibilities and sparking a sense of excitement about what lies ahead. Yet, a hundred years from now, our understanding will seem primitive compared to future science. Many concepts in physics and chemistry are already shifting as we gain a deeper understanding of the processes unfolding around us, sparking anticipation for what lies ahead.

However, much remains unexplained, whether because of ignorance, reluctance to explore, or simply because we have not yet reached the level of development needed to grasp truths beyond our current understanding. Personal exploration and discovery play a crucial role in this learning journey, empowering us to seek our truths and not rely on existing knowledge. The journey of exploration fuels our curiosity and drives us forward, instilling a sense of empowerment and curiosity.

I have always loved learning, eagerly absorbing information like a sponge. But that's only the first step in understanding the world. There is so much information that it can easily get lost in the "twists and turns" of our minds. That's why analysis is essential, sorting and organizing the knowledge into meaningful categories. Yet, you can spend endless time sorting.

And then what? The real challenge is applying and integrating your understanding into the greater Wisdom of Life.

About six months after my son was born, I had my 'flight through the tunnel' and that strange encounter with beings who, in my perception, were not human. They were ethereal, with a glow that seemed to emanate from within. The experience was filled with bliss, and I felt no desire to return to the reality of my earthly life. But I tried not to dwell on it too often or for too long because doing so would only deepen my longing to experience that bliss again and again, endlessly. These beings were unlike anything I had ever encountered before. Their presence was comforting and unsettling, a paradox I struggled to comprehend.

It was difficult for me to believe in what had happened. On the one hand, I knew it wasn't just a product of my imagination. Yet, without a scientific explanation, it felt easier to bury my "discovery" deep within my consciousness, hoping my subconscious wouldn't resurface it unexpectedly.

The only thing I truly wanted from Them was protection and guidance for my children. I made a simple request: "My children are the most precious treasures of my life. If you exist and are truly all-powerful because You are GOD, warn me when they are in danger. That is all I ask."

How strange it was that, despite not fully believing in the existence of an Egregore, a collective group mind or spirit, I entrusted it with my most precious treasures—my children. An Egregore is a thought form or collective group mind created by people with similar beliefs. The collective energy of its members sustains it. Was it blind trust? No. A part of me wanted to be blind, to cling to reason and doubt. But my subconscious had other plans. It defied logic, refusing to submit to the cold, rational thoughts I tried so hard to maintain.

For a long time, I didn't realize that even the way I phrased my request had been flawed: I had only asked for warnings but didn't fully believe in divine protection. Deep down, I entrusted no one but myself with my children's safety. And yet, God fulfilled my request despite its flawed nature and lack of complete trust. My request was flawed not because I didn't believe in divine protection but because I struggled to reconcile my faith with my sense of responsibility. I was torn between my belief in higher power and my desire to control the safety of my children.

The warnings began to come through dreams, vividly revealing what could happen to my children if I didn't act to protect them. I always arrived on time and warned my parents: "I received a message. Don't let the children do this or that. Don't leave them unsupervised while I'm away." It didn't take long to realize that my "informants" never failed me.

Still, I clung to the belief that you are You, and I am you. We can coexist, but I want nothing to do with You.

Only much later did I understand that there is no more excellent protection than the one from Above. Eventually, I surrendered fully and asked for that protection for the people I love, trusting entirely in the Forces that exist both outside and within me.

These Forces are mighty. All they ask is belief and the willingness to trust them completely.

One day, my daughter came home from a visit to the monastery with a relative. A red thread was tied around her wrist, and a black cord with knots hung around her neck. Surprised, I asked:

"What's this?"

"It's supposed to protect me from evil spirits," she said, though her tone betrayed a hint of doubt. "At least, that's what the nun told me."

I could hardly believe that a woman of faith would suggest such a form of protection.

"Tell me, do you believe in God?" I asked gently.

"Yes, I do," my daughter answered with quiet certainty.

"Every morning and every evening, you say a prayer, asking for forgiveness and protection, right?" I asked again. "And every day, 24 hours a day, you wear a cross on a chain, believing it also protects you, don't you?"

My daughter nodded in agreement.

"You know that God is everywhere. You believe that angels watch over you, right?"

"Yes, I do," she replied.

"Tell me, don't you think it's a betrayal of that trust in God to replace His constant, powerful protection with a piece of thread just because a 'spiritual figure,' a nun, told you to? Or do you think that when you sleep, God sleeps, too, and that's why you need these threads wrapped around your body to protect you from evil spirits? And who told you that such spirits have any power over you?"

My daughter listened carefully, still too young to fully grasp the logic behind my objections. But after a moment, she took off the threads and smiled.

"You're right. Who could be more powerful than Almighty? If I ask for His protection and believe in it, who else could be stronger?" she said.

People often betray their beliefs and ideals by following false convictions imposed by others. Our minds are open to specific ideas and closed to those expressed by others. Yet, ultimately, we absorb only what we choose to accept. The mind acts as a filter, capturing only the information it is tuned to receive.

This process mirrors upbringing. When a mother tells her child at the table to use a fork and knife instead of eating with their hands, many children accept the lesson and follow their parent's instructions. However, some children ignore these teachings until they are punished repeatedly or hear the same advice from others whose opinions carry more weight than their parents.

However, regarding ideology, religion, or faith, everyone must be free to make a conscious choice. The awareness of a five-year-old girl cannot be compared to the understanding of a thirty-year-old woman. Yet, no child should ever be coerced through fear, especially by invoking God or other higher powers.

***

People often say, "This is God's will" or "Perhaps God doesn't want this." Such phrases usually arise when someone feels disappointed that their dreams didn't materialize at the time they had hoped. These statements are deeply harmful, undermining a person's faith in themselves and the future they envisioned for themselves and their loved ones.

Who are we to claim to know what God desires or how He thinks about each of us? I feel nothing but pure, unconditional love from the Almighty, for God is Love. Though I've had moments of despair and doubt, they were fleeting, born merely from moments of self-pity.

Just as a mother would never wish illness, misfortune, or failure upon her child, nor would a teacher desire ignorance or poor grades for their students. How, then, can anyone proclaim that we are being punished because "this is what God wants"? It is especially disheartening when such declarations come from those who position themselves as intermediaries between God and humanity, spiritual leaders who should be a source of hope, not despair.

There was a time when I immersed myself in books on spiritual growth, parapsychology, and religion. Time and again, I encountered stories about individuals called by many names: clairvoyants, psychics, parapsychologists, mediums, spiritual leaders, metaphysicians, sorcerers, fortune-tellers, prophets, and more, each guided by a spirit from another realm, a presence with its distinct name. This sparked a question: When will I receive such a

Teacher? When will I reach the level where the door to the more profound laws of the universe opens for me?

I was in silent dialogue with someone whose name I could not know, though I knew many names ascribed to Him. I hoped for a teacher to appear in some visible form, a figure I could grasp with my mind. But from the outside, my connection seemed like speaking into a void, a conversation with emptiness. I had nothing to point to — no spiritual guide or embodied image that fit neatly within the limits of human understanding. And, for a time, that left me feeling disheartened, even lost.

But over time, clarity found me. An angel is not my teacher, not in the way I once imagined, because an angel is neither singular nor merely a spirit. The truth revealed itself: My teacher has always been God, the Almighty, the Infinite Energetic and Informational Field of the Universe. This is what I refer to as 'the Source '. Call it what you will, in whatever way your heart understands. What matters is that my connection to this Source requires no intermediaries.

It was my choice to seek knowledge directly from the Source, and in that choice, I found peace. This empowered me, filling me with a quiet certainty that I walk hand-in-hand with the One who needs no form, no name, and no face, only love and truth. This empowerment is available to all who choose to seek direct knowledge.

Mediation isn't always helpful; it can often result in miscommunication, much like the game of "broken telephone." Do you remember how it goes? We'd line up, and the first person would whisper a word into the ear of the next. That person would pass it along to the next "phone" until it reached the last person. Ultimately, everyone would reveal the word they heard, and the one who made a mistake would move to the back of the line.

Though it was a playful childhood game, it carries a more profound lesson: the more intermediaries between the Source and the intended recipient of information, the greater the chance of distortion. Each intermediary filters the message through their understanding, sometimes with errors, intentional or not. These inaccuracies can cause significant misunderstandings, leading to unintended and harmful outcomes.

For this reason, I prefer to eliminate intermediaries when receiving or sharing knowledge, regardless of the context. This choice gives me a sense of freedom, allowing me to act as the antenna, receiving the message directly, pure and unfiltered. This freedom is a powerful tool in the pursuit of knowledge and understanding.

To clarify what I said earlier, let me offer a simple example. Right now, you are reading a book I've written, which serves as a source of information.

However, how accurately this Source reflects the Original Source is something you can only speculate about, and each of you will interpret and believe its contents according to your personal beliefs. In this case, the Original Source is my life experience and accumulated knowledge.

Imagine one of your acquaintances says, "Hey, I'm reading a book by Olena Berezovska about her conversations with an Angel." This person then summarizes the content for you. Later, you meet someone else who has also read the book, but their retelling is quite different from the first. As a result, you encounter multiple versions of the same original material, each shaped by the teller's perspective, just as there will be countless opinions and interpretations of my book. But how accurately will any of these opinions and summaries reflect the original content?

If you want the most reliable information, reduce reliance on intermediaries. This approach brings clarity, as intermediaries can only serve as connectors, linking different parts of the journey that lead you to where you need to be, help you find what you seek, or introduce you to the people you are meant to meet.

The Angel supports me and appears in symbolic form whenever I need the presence of a teacher, a 'person' to guide me, like a friend or companion. In other situations, I don't see him (or Them), but I can still communicate with him on a mental level. This Angel, a manifestation of the Source, is a comforting presence in my journey, symbolizing the guidance and support always available to me directly from the Source.

***

People often tell me that I have a gift, an ability to connect effortlessly with those others either fear, tirelessly search for but cannot find, or deny even exist. Although I mentioned earlier that I once considered myself an atheist, that label doesn't fully capture the complexity of my beliefs. We were called atheists because we grew up under a communist regime, where no ideals were allowed to exist outside of the Communist Party's doctrine. There was no room for God, as Lenin, the revolutionary leader, was treated as a kind of God.

My journey from indifference to openness was tumultuous, filled with inner conflict and uncertainty. I never believed in Lenin or the Communist Party. I repeatedly refused to join, and I never became a member. While I didn't outright deny God's existence, I also struggled for a long time to embrace the idea. I wasn't hostile to faith, just indifferent. My only serious clash over religion happened with my grandmother, a woman of deep and sincere faith.

One day, I told her with all the self-assuredness of a child: "There is no God! Yuri Gagarin flew to space, and he didn't see God there. So, you're wrong, Grandma."

Her reaction was swift and passionate. "Oh, you little brat!" she snapped one of her favorite expressions. "I'll show you space! I'll show you, Gagarin! How do you know what he saw up there? And how do you know if he's telling the truth?"

Before I could say another word, she grabbed a pitchfork. In a panic, I scrambled to the nearest haystack, where I perched for hours, waiting for her to cool down. From that high perch, the world felt vast and confusing, and I learned something important: some arguments aren't meant to be won, but they can teach us valuable lessons. This incident with my grandmother taught me the value of patience, understanding, and the futility of forcing one's beliefs on others.

That was the first and last time I got into a religious dispute.

As I observed the world around me, I gradually realized that I am an inseparable part of the Universe. This realization led me to believe in the interconnectedness of all things, which transcends traditional religious boundaries. While many people don't believe in a conventional God, they place their faith in Nature and its evolutionary processes, the Earth's bioinformatical field, or the energy field of the Universe.

I once read in a book that if a person wants to be heard, they must ask for it and then wait, keeping the door of their soul or consciousness, if you prefer, wide open. Inspired by this idea, I've always remained open to positive energy, helpful information, and meaningful connections. At first, I had no clear direction, no idea which path to take or whose door to knock on. But today, I've learned that remaining open is the key. Meaningful contact can happen anytime, day or night, in any phase of life if you are open and ready to receive it. This openness has been my guiding light, leading me to unexpected and profound connections.

You've already received what I call 'information from Above' through countless channels, even if you weren't fully aware of it. This 'information' can come from insights, intuitions, or seemingly random events with deeper meaning. Often, we overlook such moments, dismissing them as mere coincidences, strange occurrences, or even miracles. But the truth is, nothing in this world is random. Every process flows seamlessly into the next, moving from one level to another in a continuous and purposeful rhythm.

***

Several years had passed since my 'flight through the tunnel,' a profound experience that opened my mind to the possibility of communication with the unknown. This experience, which I'll share later, was pivotal in my spiritual journey. One day, while cooking in the kitchen, I heard voices from the next room. No, it wasn't the voices of spirits — it was the television. The kids must have forgotten to turn it off.

The program playing was called "The Obvious and the Incredible," an intriguing show about phenomena that science can't fully explain, unusual events, and extraordinary scientific achievements. The episode ended, and I was left with a sense of wonder, having only managed to catch a demonstration of some photographs. It was like peering into a world of mystery and wonder, sparking my curiosity and igniting a flame of fascination.

The host explained that a team of scientists at a research institute had been conducting experiments. To their astonishment, a small, thin, closed loop suspended by a delicate thread would occasionally vanish from sight. It was even more remarkable that the loop's disappearance had been captured on camera.

The physicists couldn't offer a clear explanation for the phenomenon. The only hypothesis they proposed was that, at certain moments, the loop must

46

have slipped into another dimension of space and time. They suggested it might act as a conduit or antenna, briefly bridging different realities.

The photographs I saw on the television screen could have been pure fiction despite being presented by a reputable scientific institution. It wasn't the fact that the loop vanished that captivated me, nor did the photographs spark my interest. What truly struck me was a sudden thought: under the right conditions, any object, even a person, could act as a conduit or antenna.

That realization inspired me to conduct my experiment. Since I didn't have a specialized loop like the one shown in the program, I decided to use something simple: a sewing needle. I tied the needle to a piece of thread without caring about the color or length and held the end between two fingers of my right hand since I'm right-handed. I let the needle dangle freely in front of me.

But now what?

I had no clear plan, so I observed. To my surprise, the needle began to move, slowly swaying in a circular motion, following the direction of a clock's hands. At first, I thought the pulse in my hand was causing it to move. To rule that out, I steadied my arm in the most comfortable position. Yet, the needle continued its rhythmic motion.

I then wondered if my breathing could influence it. However, I needed to improvise without access to the specialized loop from the experiment. That's when the idea came to me: why not use my wedding ring? After all, a ring is just another closed loop, right? And since the ring was much heavier than the needle, it would be less likely to respond to my pulse or breath, giving me a more reliable result.

The ring began to move slowly in a circle, precisely as the needle had. But the movement stopped when I attached the ring to another object, avoiding direct contact with my hand. That's when it hit me: I was the conduit, the antenna, not the ring. Yet, if I was receiving vibrations, where were they coming from?

A thought drifted through my mind: "It feels like I'm talking to You..."

At that moment, the ring's circular motion shifted to a steady back-and-forth sway toward and away from me.

"Are you telling me this isn't just the ramblings of a madwoman?" I asked.

The answer came clearly: "Yes."

"And who am I speaking with? God?"

Once again, the response: "Yes."

It all felt utterly absurd, completely ridiculous! And yet, I couldn't ignore my past experiences: the apparition on the night my nanny passed away, the flight through the tunnel, the prophetic dreams warning me of danger to my children. On one side, I felt the resistance of someone raised to trust science and logic. But on the other hand, I was filled with curiosity and openness, the longing to understand the deeper workings of the Universe. This internal conflict was palpable, creating a tension that was hard to ignore.

Religious leaders often instill in people a sense of inferiority before God. Yet, the Bible offers beautiful words: "If the dough is holy, so is the bread." Since we are part of the Universe, part of Creation, and an expression of the Divine Idea, and therefore of God, we cannot be considered "lesser" or feel inferior to those around us, who are also integral to this whole. "And God created man in His image." This is something to celebrate, not a reason to feel like worms crawling on the earth. But back then, I didn't know or understand much.

Later, I discovered that the ancient Romans used a ring suspended on a thread to test whether food was safe, especially during long military campaigns. They would ask: "Can I eat this?" or "Is this food safe for my health?" The ring would swing toward and away from them if the answer were yes. If the answer were no, it would sway from side to side.

I started using this method to check the mushrooms we gathered from the forest. Although my mother had taught me a traditional method - throwing an onion into boiling water with the mushrooms to see if it would turn blue, I always relied on the ring for extra certainty.

I asked Them countless questions and received answers, some that unsettled me and others that completely shocked me. These answers were not just simple 'yes' or 'no' responses but often came in the form of complex insights and revelations about the nature of reality and human experience. They challenged my beliefs, expanded my understanding, and forced me to reconsider the nature of the unknown and our relationship with it. At first, I treated these exchanges as if they were just a game. But over time, I realized a few key truths: *Every question will receive an answer, but not every answer will be easy to understand or accept.*

For the answer to be accurate and close to the source, your mind must be free of preconceived notions and expected responses. During communication, you must adopt a "signal transmission — signal reception mindset," leaving aside your emotions, biases, and expectations. Alternatively, approach it as a student with a teacher: ask your question and wait patiently for the response. This openness is key to truly understanding the unknown.

If the answer you receive is uncomfortable or unpleasant, don't react with anger or skepticism. Be grateful. It means you've reached a level where your thoughts no longer interfere with the process of receiving information.

Suppose the answer turns out to be inaccurate, whether in the present or future. It might mean it was one of your preconceived ideas, or you misunderstood the message. It also serves as a reminder that humans always have free will. Life offers many paths, and you always have multiple options.

Don't turn this communication into fortune-telling or a game for amusement, especially not for the entertainment of others. I've learned to treasure these interactions as profound lessons in the unknown. I turn to this connection when I need to make an important decision but feel doubt or fear. Thanks to these exchanges, fear and doubt have become rare companions in my life.

I engage in these conversations purely for the joy they bring because that's the only way it should be.

I once read statements from several popular authors suggesting that people should not disturb "spirits" or the "otherworld" unless there is a serious need. But who, other than the individual, can honestly know how essential it is to obtain specific information, whether to make an important decision or to find peace of mind?

Of course, if communication becomes a game, the responses will reflect that it will be treated like a game. Furthermore, people tend to seek contact with whatever or whomever their imagination desires. If someone expects to connect with the spirit of a departed soul, that's precisely what they'll encounter. If they believe a genie from Aladdin's lamp will answer, a genie it shall be. And if they wish to meet an angel, complete with wings, that wish will be fulfilled, and the angel will appear with wings.

***

In communication, it's crucial to let go of fear; no one intends to harm, belittle, or judge you. Release all negative emotions. There is a law of non-interference, a philosophical principle that grants everyone the right to choose and act without external interference, regardless of how others may feel about that choice. This empowerment in making choices, whatever path you take, will be accepted. This acceptance of your choices empowers you and respects your individuality. If we find ourselves in trouble, we must ask for help, for without our request, no one will intervene. Not asking for help is still a choice to be honored with respect.

If you feel overwhelmed by challenges, fears, or negative emotions, don't hesitate to ask for help. Help will always come; when seeking help, you find the support and care you need, making you feel reassured and comforted that you are not alone in your struggles.

Fear can cause immense harm, even turning your life upside down. But with Them, you can always feel safe. Trust Them always, for in that trust, you find your security and reassurance, bringing peace and security. This trust is a beacon of hope, inspiring you to overcome your fears and confidently move forward.

Although there are no strict rules for communication, here are some suggestions to help you navigate it:

- Trust new emotions and discoveries, even if your mind feels unprepared for them.

- Do not fear anything.

- If fear arises, stay calm; do not panic.

- If you receive a warning, listen carefully before taking your next step toward discovery.

I've had a few fascinating experiences throughout my life. Once, I read that some people, under the guidance of their spiritual teachers, reach such a level of mastery that they can move through space and perceive things beyond ordinary sight — using what could be described as the vision of consciousness. For example, they are said to be able to travel within their bodies and observe how their organs function firsthand.

At that time, I didn't think I had a spiritual teacher or know how to see their internal organs from within. I wasn't even sure if I was ready for such an experience, but my curiosity won out.

As a mother, wife, homemaker, doctor, and daughter, I rarely had free time. The only moments of peace came in the evenings and late at night, when everyone in the house was asleep and a deep calm settled over everything.

One evening, as I lay on the couch, the idea began to intrigue me — how amazing it would be to see my organs from the inside, to observe every detail up close. But how could I achieve this? No one had ever taught me how. So, on a whim, I asked: "If it's not too difficult, may I experience what these enlightened people have felt?"

The answer came immediately: Yes, but under two conditions. First, I must not feel fear, as it would disrupt the experience. Second, I must not attempt to understand how the brain works or unravel the nature of consciousness, as it would distract me from the present moment. I accepted these terms.

As my body slowly relaxed, I began to feel a strange sense of duality within myself. As a gynecologist, I was particularly curious about the functioning of my ovaries. And then, suddenly, I saw them. This "vision" existed in a peculiar dimension, allowing me to simultaneously perceive them from the inside and outside. It was an odd yet pleasant sensation.

I observed the dominant ovary, where an egg was maturing, and, most importantly, everything looked perfectly normal. Afterward, I "traveled" through my blood vessels, following them upward toward the heart. What amazed me was that my movement through the organs followed the flow of my thoughts and intentions, not any predefined path or structure.

Describing the inner workings of organs seen in such an "internal" dimension is no easy task. But what I remember most vividly is the brilliance of the colors and the vibrancy of the living tissues.

Many years later, with the advent of computers, we can visualize many processes inside our bodies using specialized software. Back then, however, I had no idea what a computer was.

At last, I found myself inside my own beating heart. I watched the valves in motion, pumping blood from the atria into the ventricles. The sight was so mesmerizing, so beautiful, that I wasn't prepared to accept it as accurate, and at that moment, fear took hold of me. Panic overwhelmed my mind in the blink of an eye, and I felt an urgent need to leave this state within my body. I withdrew from the heart as quickly as I could.

Then, out of nowhere, a sharp pain shot through my chest. Panic tightened its grip: What if I die? Why is this happening?

A message followed: "You forgot the warning. You didn't trust Us to keep you safe on this journey through your body. Instead, you gave in to fear, doubting what you saw as real."

What a coward I am, I thought bitterly. I realized I wasn't ready to receive information I had previously dismissed as impossible, only to discover that it was profoundly honest in a moment of unexpected clarity.

This kind of fear isn't uncommon. People feel it when they finally confront a painful truth, like discovering a partner's infidelity, something they might have suspected all along. Yet, we resist accepting such truths until we experience them firsthand. We need to see with our own eyes and hear with our ears. That's just how we are wired.

I spent a long time reflecting on my "journey through the body," replaying every moment and image before my inner "eyes." I was grateful that I had the sense to resist the temptation to explore the workings of my brain because who knows what the consequences of such curiosity might have been.

***

Countless people call themselves clairvoyants, psychics, all-powerful fortune tellers, mediums, metaphysicians, sorcerers, and the like. I've met some of them and read books written by various individuals, including ordinary frauds working in this field.

I've always been curious about how truthful these people are, whether they genuinely possess the abilities they claim when promising miracles, healing from all illnesses, and much more. How hard is it to distinguish a genuine gift from a forgery? It can be difficult for someone inexperienced, but it becomes much more manageable with knowledge and practice.

Your body and soul become a barometer, finely tuned to detect truth from falsehood with remarkable precision. However, it's important to remember that your soul must be pure.

57

But what if you're still unsure? What should you do then?

Ask Them. By 'Them,' I refer to the spiritual entities or guides some believe in. Sometimes, all it takes is a simple 'yes' or 'no,' just one word, from Them to help you make the right decision.

Numerous textbooks on developing specialized senses and enhancing existing ones exist. Readers and practitioners decide how effective they are. An entire field of study, known as mentalism, explores the hidden potential of human consciousness. Mentalists argue that nothing is genuinely supernatural; much of what seems impossible lies within the mind's reach.

With the right exercises, such as meditation, visualization, and energy work, one can master almost anything: healing, prophecy, communication with spirits, traveling through space and time, or performing magic tricks. This journey of self-discovery and empowerment is open to all willing to explore their intuitive potential, offering a sense of empowerment that can inspire and motivate.

The primary condition for attaining mastery is the absence of resistance. People must remain open, fully aligned with their goals, and free from inner conflict. This journey is not without its challenges, but with honesty with oneself, which involves acknowledging one's strengths and weaknesses, persistence, and consistency in practice, one can overcome these obstacles and unlock their intuitive potential.

I didn't have time for dedicated practice to sharpen my perceptions when working with people or objects. Yet, when the need arose, I could sense and see things others could not. Often, while working with patients, my hands acted as a natural "X-ray," allowing me to visualize the internal structure of an organ. A person's skin would become like a screen, projecting the condition of the underlying organs onto its surface.

Over time, my fingertips developed the ability to detect even the subtlest shifts in body temperature and sense the flow of bioenergy, skills that proved invaluable when diagnosing malignant tumors. A malignant tumor is like a black hole in space: it absorbs energy but uses almost none.

Even a tiny cluster of malignant cells, living and growing according to their autonomous laws, can be identified as a cold spot, draining energy from the surrounding cells and tissues.

One day, I asked Them to let me experience the kind of energy some healers use. I didn't know how they harnessed this energy or directed it into their hands. The answer came instantly: as soon as I relaxed, I felt a growing flow of white energy, like a brilliant white light, pouring from the top of my head and streaming into my hands. It was a moment of profound wonder and awe, a glimpse into the extraordinary potential of the human mind, a feeling that can intrigue and fascinate.

My hands began to feel like they were swelling, expanding like oversized boxing gloves. The sensation was so intense that it became difficult to keep my fists closed. I sat there, mesmerized, staring at my hands in disbelief.

My husband sat beside me and asked, "What's going on?"

"I don't know," I replied. "What's happening to my hands?"

I opened my palms and held them facing each other. A powerful stream of energy flowed between them, like two plates of a transformer humming with charge. Intrigued, my husband slipped his hand between my palms, and the hair on his arm immediately stood on end.

Startled, Yuri quickly pulled his hand back. "What was that?" he asked, wide-eyed.

"Nothing special — just energy," I replied with a grin.

It took a few minutes for the energy flow to subside. Gradually, my hands relaxed and stopped "burning" with that strange, potent energy.

But what lingered was a deep sense of satisfaction. I now understand what some healers feel during their sessions.

Don't rush to assume that you lack any extraordinary senses. It's often we who close the door to that realm of perception. Take the time to reflect on your past experiences. You'll likely discover many instances when your inner senses guide you, offering insights, helping you overcome challenges, or steering you in the right direction. This reflection can make you feel introspective and contemplative.

Consider keeping a dedicated notebook to record anything you perceive as a signal or a helping hand from Above. Over time, you'll realize that you've been receiving answers to your questions all along — it's just that you weren't always open to recognizing them.

You can also ask God to help you find your doorway into this remarkable world of the unknown. This world exists both within and beyond the boundaries of your consciousness. And you'll find that the answer is always "yes."

***

Communicating with an Angel is always a joy; it evokes a sense of light and warmth. The Angel's presence brings comfort and peace, wrapping you in tranquility. And how precious and vital that support becomes during life's difficult moments.

I once had a close friendship with someone whose opinion I deeply valued. He often told me, "Our friendship is like a massive stone boulder, solid and unbreakable, just like you. Nothing and no one can ever destroy it." I believed his words. But time has no regard for absolutes; it resists rigidity and certainty. The universe, however, responds not to what we merely declare but to the thoughts that carry the most powerful energy within us.

There was a woman I knew who, whenever the topic of her friends' divorces came up, would say bitterly, "I will never, ever marry a divorced man, especially one with children, and certainly not someone older." But by focusing so intensely on what she feared most, her "never" became her reality sooner than she expected. She ended up marrying an older, divorced man with three children. Whether she married him for love or his wealth and status is her matter, but in the end, she received exactly what she had placed so much mental energy on.

62

This is why when people assure me of things with words like "never," "nothing," "no one," "forever," "for the rest of my life," "I promise," or "once and for all," I can't help but smile. Life always has surprises in store. When someone fixates on something with such force, they are already moving toward that reality, whether they realize it or not.

Circumstances soon took a turn, and my "friend" began to fear interacting with me. He struggled to understand some of my actions and words. Deeply religious, he was bound by the tenets of his traditional faith, making it difficult for him to accept that I, a person far from spiritual, could receive insights directly from the Source.

I was too candid and careless in some of my remarks, eventually leading to a hurtful comment: "Are you sure you're okay? Maybe you should see a doctor?" The implication was a psychiatrist.

Other uncomfortable moments also occurred, tied to his personal and family life, as he navigated a challenging period.

I am not gifted in expressing my thoughts elegantly and vaguely enough to avoid being dismissed as irrational by a skeptic or cast as mysterious by a contemplative soul. I speak plainly because I feel deeply and. There is already too much ambiguity and pretense in human interaction, and from that spring, misunderstandings, resentment, and envy. This makes people believe that while some have no problems, others are weighed down by them.

When I finally understood that the "solid, unbreakable stone boulder" of friendship between us had never truly existed, I blamed it for its collapse. I believed it was my fault, my inadequacy, my failure to understand others, and my tendency to bring problems rather than joy into people's lives. The pain of that realization was unbearable. I wept as if I had buried someone I loved dearly as if I were mourning the death of a cherished connection.

But alongside that sorrow, something new began to stir within me. A quiet yet persistent voice urged me to say: "I am not as broken, foolish, or unworthy as I have been made to feel. I am not without spirit, nor am I sick or lost." This self-realization was a turning point, a moment of empowerment that fueled my growing need to reclaim and understand my life because it had not always been kind to me.

On the one hand, I am happy and find joy in the little things. No matter how small, these moments of pleasure are like beacons of light amid life's challenges. But on the other hand, my life had also been marked by hardships and even moments of profound drama. This led me to questions: Why? What had it all caused? Where did it come from? And why did sorrow so often accompany joy? These questions sparked a journey of self-discovery and understanding that I invite you to join.

Out of nowhere, I felt an overwhelming urge to write a book titled "My Path to Truth." I had no idea what it would be about, but every morning, as if summoned by unseen forces, I would wake early, sit at my typewriter, and begin to type, words flowing effortlessly as if they bypassed my mind entirely.

Before long, I realized I was merely a conduit, an antenna receiving thoughts from somewhere beyond my consciousness. It was like I was being guided by a higher power, a force leading me to share these profound insights. Within a month, the book, nearly one hundred pages long, was complete. It contained everything that had been stirring within me: reflections on the relationship between the self and God or the Universe and explorations of human emotions and experiences — love, motherhood, friendship, and much more.

Just as the book neared completion, I had a dream early one morning that felt more like a message than a mere dream.

I have always loved taking photographs, especially of children. Their joyful faces fill the pages of our thick family albums, capturing moments of pure happiness. I sat on a bed in a dream, flipping through these familiar photographs. Suddenly, one picture caught my eye - a rare color photograph, as such photos were a luxury at the time. There I was, captured in vibrant detail, sitting on fresh, bright green grass, my head turned slightly toward the photographer. On my head rested a wreath of breathtaking beauty. This dream was filled with wonder and curiosity, a feeling we all experience when encountering something extraordinary.

Surprised, I said:

"I don't remember this moment... When was this taken? Who took it? And where?"

A voice responded:

"Would you like to see that moment?"

Still bewildered, I asked:

"Is that even possible? Can you return to the exact moment when this photo was taken?"

The answer came gently but with certainty:

"With Us, everything is possible. Nothing is impossible."

In that instant, the photograph projected onto the wall, and the images began to move. Frames shifted rapidly, rewinding into the past at incredible speed, like a film reel spinning backward in fast motion.

I find myself in a place of breathtaking beauty, a lush, green meadow surrounded by towering mountains crowned with glistening snow. Tall, graceful trees, unlike any I've ever seen, sway gently, and the soft melodies of birdsong mingle with the subtle music of nature itself, creating a symphony of peace.

I sit quietly on the grass, my hair draping over my shoulders. I'm dressed in simple white linen, my bare feet resting on the cool earth. Where am I? Why am I here?

Then I hear a voice, calm and steady:

"Are you ready?"

I looked around, wondering who spoke to me. To my left, nature unfolds in all its splendor, vivid, serene, and untouched. I glance over my shoulder and see, far below, people busy in the forest. They load carts with firewood, and I spot clay pots filled with milk and freshly baked bread among the bundles. I observe them from a distance, as if from another realm, watching them talk, laugh, and share a meal. "That's Earth," I think, "down there."

Then I turn back, and in front of me stands a translucent wall stretching infinitely into the sky. At first, it seems solid and thick, but the longer I look, the more fragile and delicate it appears, like a veil between worlds. Yet beyond it, I see only light. It may be even more beautiful on the other side. Then, I noticed a small door embedded in the wall, as if it's only temporary. Where does it lead?

"Are you ready?" the voice asks again, gentle yet persistent.

That's when I realized I was not alone. An Angel stands a short distance away, cloaked entirely in black. But I know it wasn't him who spoke. If not him, then who?

I gaze and see a radiant orb of pure white light hovering above me. Its brightness is overwhelming, yet it doesn't hurt my eyes; it feels familiar as if I've encountered it before.

"Why is this light here?" I ask softly. "Can't it move aside just a little?"

"With Us, anything is possible," the answer comes, calm and reassuring. The orb shifts slightly to the side as if responding to my request with ease.

"What does all of this mean?" I whispered, turning to the Angel. And in that moment, I feel it — an undeniable presence. The light isn't just watching me; it is listening. It understands me without words, waiting, patient, and silent, as if everything I need to know is already within me, ready to surface when I am prepared to receive it.

The Angel remains silent, his smile calm and knowing. Suddenly, a breathtakingly beautiful wreath appears in his hands, woven from extraordinary flowers that seem to glow from within. It isn't just a single wreath — it's a series of interconnected ones. The first three layers are made from a vibrant blend of yellow and violet flowers. Beyond them, more miniature wreaths follow, crafted primarily from pale yellow, almost white blossoms. How many layers are there? I don't know, but it feels endless. From the crown of this creation flows a powerful stream of white light, radiant and pure. I am mesmerized by its beauty.

The Angel steps closer, and at that moment, I realize the wreath is meant for me. A flicker of uncertainty passes through me; it looks so intricate and grand that it must be cumbersome. How will I bear its weight? But with graceful ease, the Angel gently places the wreath on my head.

The moment it touches me, a wave of indescribable bliss washes over me — the same overwhelming ecstasy I felt in the tunnel leading toward the light. It's as if the light enfolds me, cradling me in love, care, and protection pure bliss.

"Are you ready?" the voice asks again, for the third time.

I turn to the left and see myself sitting on a bed, watching my image reflected on the wall. In that instant, I finally understood when and where the photograph was taken. But the meaning behind the question — "*Are you ready?*" — still eludes me.

I woke up filled with a profound sense of relief. I am light as a feather, free from every burden.

At different stages of my life, I've had other answers to that question. At first, I would say, "I am ready." Ready for what? I believed I was prepared for death. In my understanding, death is simply a transition, a passage from one level of existence to another. So why fear it? I felt sure that if my time came, I could leave without hesitation despite having children, loved ones, dreams, passions, and so much more. Are you ready?

But as I live longer and gain more wisdom from life's lessons, I find myself answering differently: "No, I am not ready to die." Not because I am afraid but because I don't want to. In this life, I have my children, my loved ones, my passions, my dreams, and countless things I am not ready to leave behind. I have not yet savored life to the point where I could say, with peace and relief, "I am ready to go."

There are still so many joyful moments to live, future days filled with beauty, love, and discovery. I have books to write, paintings to draw, and pictures to capture. I dream of meeting fascinating people, traveling to extraordinary places, and experiencing everything life offers. There is still so much ahead of me. Life is a calling, and I want to embrace it with all its joys and wonders.

Imagine yourself driving a car, traveling from one place to another. You don't know exactly where your destination is, how far it is, or what it looks like because you've never been there before. All you have is a map showing the distance and the general direction. There's a main road leading you toward your final stop. How quickly you get there depends on your speed and ability to stay on course.

Now, picture that this final destination is the last day of your life. You know it will come, eventually, but how fast you arrive depends on the pace at which you live. Some people speed through life at a breakneck pace, rushing past everything and everyone, barely noticing the world around them. Others move slowly, like a steady, deliberate, and patient turtle.

But what if you allow yourself to make stops along the way instead of rushing or crawling? You pause to admire the landscapes, explore cities and villages, meet people, and savor each encounter. You may even take unexpected detours, wandering off the main path to discover hidden places worth exploring. Or you could choose an entirely different route: one that is more scenic, exciting, or even more challenging, filled with obstacles and surprises.

And what happens if you do? Nothing terrible; your final destination isn't going anywhere. You will reach it eventually, no matter which route you take.

So why not make that last day a joyful one? A day filled with peace because, along the way, you created countless meaningful moments and happy memories. Most importantly, you'll carry the deep satisfaction of knowing that your journey through life was extraordinary, an adventure uniquely your own, filled with beauty, challenges, and moments worth cherishing.

After completing my book, I shared only five copies with people whose opinions mattered most. Each one gave me glowing, positive feedback. Yet, I hesitated to publish it. Something felt unfinished as if an essential piece was still missing. Years passed before I revisited the text, enriching it with new insights and experiences. My journey toward truth is far from over; many discoveries, encounters, and meaningful events are still ahead.

When will I complete "My Path to Truth"? Perhaps when, alongside this book, I have brought to life all the creations I've envisioned and those who have chosen me as their vessel. These works, expressed through books, paintings, photographs, and other mediums, are waiting to emerge through the canvas of my life. Only then will my journey feel complete when all has found its place.

***

Every person faces difficult periods in life. While we may endure financial or material hardships for long stretches, even a lifetime, emotional struggles and moral crises can destabilize us for much longer, leaving deep and painful scars on the soul.

How often have you thought, "I can't go on like this," overwhelmed by exhaustion and questioning the meaning of life? Friends and acquaintances say, "I can't live like this anymore. I don't want to live like this!" Their words were always tinged with bitterness, anger, despair, and hopelessness.

I, too, have experienced moments when I didn't want to go on living. But I never seriously considered ending my life; I'm a deeply responsible person. I knew that I couldn't allow my children, my loved ones, and those close to me to carry the burden of such a loss. I had no right to inflict that kind of pain, disappointment, and tragedy on their lives, knowing they would carry the weight of that grief forever.

Sadly, many people, consumed by depression and despair, become blind to the support and care around them. They struggle to see that those who love them, though not always able to express it fully, are not indifferent. They, too, suffer, frustrated by their inability to help in the way they wish they could. But it's crucial to remember that there is help available.

Seeking professional support or even opening up to a trusted friend can make a significant difference in overcoming these struggles.

One night, I had a dream that brought me a sense of relief and hope, putting an end to any lingering thoughts of suicide.

In the dream, I was at a train station, preparing for a long journey. I didn't know exactly where we were headed, which city we were traveling to, or what time we would depart. I asked my husband and children to retrieve the luggage, urging them to hurry so we wouldn't miss the train, while I ran ahead to the platform.

A long train stood waiting on the first platform. I approached the last carriage, and to my surprise, it had no windows, just a single door. "How strange," I thought. "How can people travel in a carriage without windows? Won't they suffocate?"

Curiosity got the better of me, and I walked up to the door at the end of the carriage, hoping to get a glimpse inside. Standing on the steps like a gatekeeper, the conductor blocked my way. However, I noticed narrow compartments, like shelves, where passengers lay quietly as if waiting for the train to depart.

"Do people travel like this the whole way?" I wondered, unsettled by the thought. The idea of such a journey struck me as deeply uncomfortable, even eerie.

I looked around, searching for my husband and children. Anxiety washed over me; I was afraid we'd miss the train. And just a second or two later, the train began to move, slowly picking up speed. "Well, I missed it," I thought. But then I heard a Voice: "It's not your time yet. You'll catch your train."

"What time is it?" I asked. I lifted my head and saw a clock on a pole beside me. The hour and minute hands were perfectly aligned, both pointing to twelve. Or was it zero? Is this the end or the beginning? I wondered. Each person may interpret it differently; some might see it as the end of life, while others might see it as the start of something new.

And what if it's the beginning of a new life? If that's the case, then it's terrific that the train, which wasn't meant for me, has already left. Let it go.

We are all rushing somewhere, rushing to work, a date, the store, trying to get this or that done. But Festina lente - "Hurry but slowly." Take the time to notice the beauty of the world around you and realize how wonderful life is.

I remember the time I tried desperately to catch a departing bus. I wasn't late for work, but I didn't want to wait another ten minutes for the next one. Determined to save time, I climbed a steep, slippery hill, hoping to take a shortcut to the bus stop. Just as I reached within a meter of the bus, I tripped and fell hard onto the wet asphalt. My tights tore, my dress got stained, and blood trickled from my scraped elbows and knees. What did I gain from all that rushing? Nothing. I had to return home, clean up, change my clothes, and, limping in pain, make my way back to the bus stop.

We often end up in dramatic or tragic situations simply because we rush toward them. Forget fatalism - it doesn't exist. People are born to live, not to die, even though life inevitably moves us toward death from the moment we take our first breath. Yet, life will fight against death as long as it can resist until our mission on Earth is complete.

Regrettably, many people abandon their mission prematurely because they fail to value their lives. Why must they hold on to it if they don't see the worth of living? That is why so many perish; they stop appreciating the gift of life. It's essential to understand that life is valuable, and by recognizing this, we can find the strength to hold on and appreciate every moment.

**

The Angel has guided me through some of the most difficult moments in my life. One of the most challenging was our family's move to Canada. While the decision was voluntary, we longed for positive change and a brighter future for our children; it was also born out of necessity. Life in Ukraine had become so complex that we were barely surviving, cutting back on everything and denying ourselves the simplest comforts to get by.

In larger cities, where food supplies were relatively stable and varied, people didn't experience the same hardship. But in smaller towns and rural areas, where life depended heavily on the timely payment of wages, things were far worse. Salaries were delayed for eight to nine months at a time. We worked eight to ten hours daily, only waiting another five or six hours in endless lines for essential groceries. Any remaining free time was devoted to tending small plots of land outside the city, where we grew fruits and vegetables to preserve for the winter.

The situation only worsened. Political and economic chaos fueled rampant corruption. Those in power grew wealthy almost overnight, exploiting access to state funds and resources, while ordinary people sank deeper into poverty. The gap between the rich and the poor widened, leaving many struggling to survive.

Leaving the country where I was born and raised was incredibly hard. Saying goodbye to family and friends and the familiar life I had known to start fresh in a foreign land was overwhelming. What frightened me the most was losing my connection to my roots. This fear weighed heavily on my heart, filling my mind with complex thoughts and emotions. I couldn't imagine the moment when I would leave my hometown and my parents, knowing there was a possibility I might never return. In the days leading up to our departure, I cried almost every day, overcome by the pain of the impending separation.

Just a few days before we were scheduled to leave, I had a dream. In it, I found myself at an airfield next to a small airport. Piles of suitcases and bags were stacked, ready to be loaded onto the plane, and a long line of people waited at the security gate. My turn finally came to present my documents and ticket. But the weight of it all became too much; I stepped aside, sat down on the grass, and began to sob uncontrollably.

"Calm down, stop crying," a voice gently urged from nearby. But I buried my face in my hands and continued to weep, unable to contain the sorrow that overwhelmed me.

But the voice continued:

"Listen, child, you are not losing anything or anyone. Look at me. I have lived countless lives, taken on many roles, and worked in various professions. But every change was for the better. I never lost those I was meant to keep; my true friends stayed with me. Those who only loved me with words drifted away, making room for those who truly cared. I have never lost; I have only gained more with every transformation. And so will you: you are not losing anything. Your life is shifting to offer you more - new friends, new experiences, and new heights to reach. Be at peace, child."

I uncovered my face, lifted my head, and looked at the person speaking. It was the Angel I had seen many times before, once again dressed in black. His eyes shone with kindness, and in his gaze, I felt warmth and calm settle over me like a gentle embrace. His words were impossible to doubt; they carried a truth that resonated deep within me.

At last, I felt peace. I stood, brushed off my tears, and walked toward the airport gate.

That morning, when I woke, I wrote a poem called "Angel" in Ukrainian.

A strange dream came to me one night,
As if I were set to take flight,
Alone by customs, gripped by fear,
My heart in pieces, my eyes in tears.

I bid farewell to those I love,

To friends and family, those I trust.
I left behind my cherished land,
With weary soul and trembling hands.

Tears poured like rivers wild and deep,
No matter how I tried, I'd weep.
But through my sobs, a voice rang clear,
A soothing whisper drawing near:

"Calm yourself, child, don't despair,
You lose nothing, have no fear.
This is your chance to start anew,
And greater blessings wait for you.

I've lived many lives, worn many names,
Known joy, known sorrow, loss, and gain.
I've had my share of love's embrace,
And tasted happiness' sweetest grace.

Remember this, my dearest one:
What you sow among the crowd
Will return to you in kind,
Multiplied, full and proud.

True friends will stay, they always do,
Their love will guide you through and through.
But those who loved you with empty words
Will leave, as they should, unheard.

Hold no grudge and let it go,
Don't mourn what fate will not bestow.
Some hearts, though they claim to love,
Are shrouded by falsehoods from above.

Not all can conquer pride and spite,
Or hide the envy they invite.
Some let their shadows guide their way,
And cast their joy and hope away.

You made no wrong step on your quest,
For you sought goodness in the rest.
But sadly, with the light you sought,
Their hidden darkness, too, you caught.

So, leave behind the hurt and pain,
And let no bitterness remain.
Do not mourn those who turned away,
They had no place with you today.

Believe, sweet child, that brighter days
Await you on life's winding ways.
Be calm, be hopeful, stay sincere,
And live your truth without fear.

Look around — the sun still shines,
Its warmth flows gently, soft, divine.
Life is beautiful, so let your soul
Sing freely, joyfully, and whole."

I opened my hands, raised tired eyes,
And saw the man who spoke so wise.
Though unknown to me, his gaze was kind,
His smile brought peace to heart and mind.

His eyes shone bright with gentle grace,
And at his sight, my fears erased.
I stood in silence, lost and still,
Yet deep within, I felt fulfilled.

A heavyweight slipped from my soul,
And all my burdens ceased to roll.
I woke and knew, without a doubt -
An angel had sought me out.

He came to me that night in need,
To rescue me from doubt and grief,
To ease the pain that clouded my way,
And teach me hope for another day.

He came as a friend, a teacher, a guide,
To walk with me through life's rough tides.
Oh, how blessed I am to know,
That my guardian angel walks where I go.

Three days before our departure, I met with the
editor of a local newspaper. He had once been a student
of my father, who had played a key role in helping him
become the editor of a well-regarded publication.

During our conversation, we discussed publishing a few of my poems.

At one point, the editor asked if he could print a farewell message for my family, wishing us well on our move to another country. I agreed but on one condition: the message would be published only after we had left.

To my dismay and frustration, several people called me on the morning of our departure to say that an article about me had appeared in that day's newspaper. To my shock, it wasn't just a farewell note; it was framed as an interview I had supposedly given. In it, I was quoted as saying that I felt no attachment to the friends and family I was leaving behind and that I was eagerly starting a new life in Canada without regret.

The article left me and my loved ones deeply stunned and hurt. Its content was a complete fabrication, bearing no resemblance to the truth. In my conversation with the editor, I expressed the exact opposite — how heart-wrenching it was to leave behind the people I cherished.

My father called the editor, his former student, and asked, "Why did you do this?" To this day, I don't know whose reputation the journalist was trying to boost with his lies. I spent half the day in tears, overwhelmed with sadness and disappointment. Yet, amid the heartbreak, something beautiful happened: people who knew and respected me reached out, called, and even came in person to say their goodbyes.

The Angel's words rang true: my real friends remained beside me. Despite the distance that now separated us, we stayed connected not only through letters but also through joyful reunions. And new friends and acquaintances soon entered my life. In the end, I gained far more than I ever lost.

Years later, five or six years after our departure, I received an unexpected letter from that same editor. His career had fallen apart; he had been dismissed from his position and let go from the newspaper entirely. In his letter, he asked me for a favor: to help his son find a job in Canada. The irony was striking, but I couldn't help but feel that life has a way of balancing things, always revealing the truth in time.

***

Life in Canada wasn't easy at first. The absence of work and money filled us with fear for the future. We arrived with only a few suitcases and around two hundred Canadian dollars, starting our new life from scratch. But we didn't succumb to the challenges. Despite the hardships, we found our footing, caring for our children and each family member. Alongside the

84

struggles of survival, we made room for joy; our celebrations were filled with laughter and happiness, not just the grind of endless workdays.

The Angel was my constant support, especially when doubt crept into my heart, making happiness feel distant. One day, exhausted, I drifted into sleep. In my dream, I was driving through the night, the road ahead barely visible in the dark. I glanced into the rearview mirror, and the Angel's eyes were watching me from the back seat, calm and kind, assuring me that I was not alone.

"I'm tired," I whispered. "So tired. It's hard to believe in anything good anymore."

"Everything will be all right, trust me," the Angel said gently. "Hardships are only temporary. They will weigh on you today, but tomorrow, they'll be gone."

"But whenever I solve one problem, another one follows," I murmured.

The Angel smiled. "And what kind of problems do you have?"

"I don't know... all kinds," I replied, feeling overwhelmed. "From financial struggles to the stress of adapting to a new country, it feels like a never-ending cycle of problems."

"Give me an example," he encouraged.

"Little things, one thing after another. I want my life to change," I admitted.

"Then change it," the Angel said softly. "Who else but you know what kind of life you dream of? Who else knows what you truly want?"

"No one," I whispered. "Only I know."

"Then believe in yourself," the Angel said warmly. "And trust me, everything will work out. So well, you'll be amazed by just how beautiful your life has become one day." This belief in yourself is the key to unlocking the beauty in your life.

The Angel smiled and vanished.

I worked tirelessly, spent days at the clinic, managed countless tasks, and spent nights at a small café tucked inside a gas station. In front of me was a vast black window, a portal into the night, a constant reminder of my challenges. I would stare into its darkness and whisper, "One day, this window will disappear from my life, just like this job. And with them, many of my problems will fade away."

And that's precisely what happened. Before long, I stopped working nights, and the black window became a memory. I could finally sleep peacefully in my bed, savoring the comfort of rest, no longer standing behind a counter, serving hot, fragrant coffee to lonely travelers passing through the night.

My life feels like a thick, well-worn book, with each page-turning effortlessly and full of intrigue and joy. There are no dull moments I wish I could cut out or skip over. Every chapter matters, and each experience, good and bad, has meaning.

And your life should be no different.

Believe me and believe the Angel; everything in life is temporary. Problems have a way of resolving themselves, often without you even realizing it. The hard times don't last forever because something good always follows sooner or later if you can wait for it.

To remind yourself of the abundance of good in your life, grab a notebook and start jotting down moments from your past that brought you joy and pleasure. Pull out your photo albums, watch your family videos, and you'll quickly realize that life hasn't been as bleak as it sometimes seems.

Select the best photos, especially those where you're smiling or laughing genuinely. Carry those images with you, even if it's just one. If you could laugh so wholeheartedly at the moment the photo was taken, what's stopping you from embracing that same joy today?

***

Financial hardship is a significant issue for many people. There's a saying: "Why is he poor? Because he's a fool. Why is he a fool? Because he's poor." These harsh words vividly illustrate the vicious cycle that traps many, with few able to break free.

Despite my excellent education and strong work ethic, I found myself in a situation where financial success seemed elusive. Loved people often questioned me, 'You're so smart and educated, but why are you still struggling financially?' These words, though well-intentioned, usually felt like a thorn in my side. I'm sure many of you have experienced similar situations where your potential and abilities are questioned because of your financial situation.

At times, such compliments felt like a thorn in my side. On the one hand, there was truth and goodwill in their words. On the other hand, where was the logic in it? What was the real obstacle? Who or what was holding me back?

For a long time, I grappled with conflicting emotions. Many spiritual leaders have taught me that it is sinful to desire material things if one seeks spiritual growth. I genuinely resisted the temptation to live a better or wealthier life, fully aware that many others lived in far worse conditions than I did. I often asked the Angel if seeking more than just spiritual advancement, including financial and material prosperity, was wrong. The answer was always the same: there is no sin in this; it is encouraged. Yet, I found it difficult to accept, convinced I must be misunderstanding something. This internal conflict, this tug-of-war between what I was taught and what I felt, can be a heavy burden.

One Christmas, I found myself in church. After the service, I noticed a nun wearing a stunning mink coat just by the entrance. In comparison, my old coat looked downright shabby. What struck me most was that this nun, who had voluntarily renounced worldly life and all its temptations, was adorned with one of those temptations: a luxurious garment made from expensive fur. I asked a fellow parishioner how appropriate it was for a spiritual figure to wear such costly attire. In response, I received justifications: the coat could have been a gift from the nun's relatives; she was elderly and might feel cold, thus needing a warm coat.

But couldn't she have sold the coat, sacrificing that luxury, and used the proceeds to help those in need? To buy Christmas gifts for orphans?

Modern spiritual leaders and guides harness the latest technologies to spread their teachings and reach a broader audience rapidly. There's nothing inherently wrong with this. However, many leaders generate significant personal income while promoting their philosophies. Is there a contradiction in this? How can we reconcile traditional, mainly orthodox, religious teachings with these spiritual figures' luxurious, almost regal lifestyles? This is where the need for questioning societal norms becomes apparent, empowering us to challenge the status quo and seek our truths.

Conversely, I have met several spiritual mentors who advocate for spiritual growth while living in dire poverty. They explain their unfortunate financial situations by asserting that material wealth is incompatible with spiritual advancement. Yet, they do not hesitate to buy lottery tickets or solicit donations from their followers.

So, is it truly wrong to aspire to spiritual development and financial security?

An angel awaited me on the shore of a serene, azure sea. The tranquil waters mirrored the golden rays of the rising sun.

"What beauty!" I whispered in awe. The Angel smiled softly, saying nothing.

"I have so many questions I've wanted to ask you!" I began eagerly.

"Yet many of your questions are answered not only by me," the Angel said calmly, radiating a sense of tranquility.

"And not always with words," I added. "Tell me, what's troubling me?"

"Troubling you?" The Angel tilted his head, a hint of surprise in his expression. "Do you truly believe you have a problem?"

"I often hear that we should be content with what we already have and that wanting more, especially material things like money, is almost sinful."

The Angel replied, "That's a misconception. People are meant to dream and aspire to more, for their dreams play a vital role in creation. Those who are fulfilled and joyful generate immense positive energy, which spreads and elevates others around them. Your positive thoughts can indeed impact the lives of others. But they will transform your life first. And because your life touches many others, that transformation will ripple outward and affect them too." This personal transformation, this journey of self-discovery and growth, is a powerful force that can inspire others.

"So, my positive thoughts can impact the lives of others?"

"Yes. But they will transform your life first. And because your life touches many others, that transformation will ripple outward and affect them too."

The Angel gestured toward the calm sea. "Do you see how the smooth surface reflects the light?"

"Yes," I whispered, mesmerized by the beauty before me.

"You said 'Beautiful' because this serene seascape evokes pleasant emotions within you. But are you aware that beneath the surface, the sea teems with unseen, turbulent life? Does that mean we should dismiss the calm waters above as a mere illusion?"

"But a sunrise over the sea is breathtaking in its own right, regardless of what stirs beneath the depths," I replied.

"Exactly. And so it is with life, no matter what lies beneath the surface. People see what they choose to see. For some, every day will feel extraordinary; for others, dull and forgettable."

"But you still haven't answered my question: what is my problem?"

The Angel gave a knowing smile and asked,

"You already know the answer. So why not tell me yourself?"

***

Reflecting on my journey, I've often pondered the question, 'What is wrong with me?' particularly in the face of setbacks. I was a high achiever in school and university, consistently ranking among the top students. My professional trajectory mirrored this success, characterized by rapid advancement and accolades. Even in new roles, I quickly climbed the ranks, fostering the growth of those around me.

Yet, despite my achievements, I often encountered systems that remained inaccessible, no matter how much knowledge, hard work, or professional development I brought to the table. Connections and personal endorsements have always played a crucial role in any society. Many systems, especially financial ones, are built and sustained through these networks of influence.

Society, governmental bodies, private organizations, political institutions, and educational establishments all operate as pyramids. Entering these systems often requires the endorsement of one or more existing members, ideally those at the top. Securing such backing can be challenging, though it can sometimes be bought or acquired through a chain of referrals from other systems.

Every system, however, imposes its limitations, whether moral, financial, or material. Continuous growth often requires adapting to new systems or building your subsystems or frameworks. But creating something new isn't always easy.

Society itself is just another system—one that doesn't always welcome the so-called "black sheep," the ones who stand out, the ones who don't fit the mold.

Many people ask themselves: Why, despite all my honest efforts, does my life never seem to improve? Who is to blame? I often hear that there must be someone or something at fault. And just as often, I hear people say, "I'm just a failure, end of story."

It's important to remember that setbacks are not a sign of failure. They are simply part of the journey. There are only two fundamental reasons for your setbacks:

You overlook the positives in your life, focusing only on the negatives. When all your attention is on what's going wrong, you block yourself from seeing progress, however small. If you want to improve your life, you need to actively track positive changes and achievements, no matter how minor they may seem.

You are stuck in a system that no longer supports your growth. This system may have become a stagnant routine, or perhaps you never learned how to leverage it to your benefit. If it no longer serves you, it's time to leave. If you don't know how or when to walk away or feel unprepared, start working toward your exit today. Prepare yourself step by step to move on when the moment comes.

***

Have you ever considered that most people function like robots, following a pre-set program installed in their minds and control centers by others who are often just as programmed by society? Our brains can absorb and store information but usually do so without critical analysis.

Our lives are programmed from the moment we are born. Children are taught everything, good and bad, and often, parents pass down the lessons they learned from their parents. These lessons are shaped by personal experiences, which are not always positive or helpful.

I often heard my parents say, "You can't have this or that because many other children don't have it." My parents were not poor; they held stable government jobs with good salaries, had a flat, and were satisfied with the security their lives provided. Yet, their contentment was rooted in maintaining stability, not exploring new possibilities.

In school, we were taught that everyone should be equal and that aspiring to wealth was wrong, as it contradicted communist moral codes and proletarian ideals. Yet some of my classmates were children of high-ranking officials and communist leaders, and they often boasted about their foreign toys. They could casually spend money on pastries at the school café and ride to and from school in government cars, chauffeured by their parents' drivers.

When I asked why some had so much while others had almost nothing, my parents often responded with bitterness. They would tell me that injustice is simply a part of the world, and that the wealthy were nothing more than swindlers and thieves. Honest people, they insisted, shouldn't complain or demand more but should be content with what they have.

At the same time, the teachers who taught us to live honestly and to work selflessly for the nation's good rather than for personal gain didn't hesitate to accept expensive gifts from certain parents. For these parents, securing good grades for their lazy, unruly children mattered more than merit. In truth, many things could be bought with money or lavish gifts.

This was the lesson we learned outside the classroom through everyday life examples. Ideals remained noble words on paper, but reality often strayed far from them.

My parents often told me I should focus on school first, then on college, secure a good job at an institution, work diligently until retirement, and only after that, think about rest. To them, this was the essence of a stable life, even though their lives had never known stability.

They lived through Stalin's repressions, World War II, the post-war devastation and hunger, and the collapse of the very country where they were born, raised, and spent most of their lives.

Stability is akin to death; it signifies the absence of movement. Proper stability has never existed in this world. Believing that holding a government job with a regular paycheck provides lasting security is nothing more than a comforting illusion. *Life is in constant motion*. What exists today may be gone tomorrow, including that government institution you thought would last forever.

I once lived across from a massive plant that fulfilled numerous military contracts. I still vividly remember the long streams of people making their way to work early each morning. Tens of thousands were employed there, earning relatively stable wages, and stability seemed never to end. My sister also worked at the plant.

But then, almost overnight, the Soviet Union vanished from the world map, along with the significant military contracts that kept the plant running. Thousands of factories and plants scattered across what were now the remains of a collapsed country suffering the same fate. Those with access to financial resources quickly built fortunes, taking advantage of the chaos and the absence of oversight. Yet, these fortunate few were rare exceptions.

Thousands of workers were cast out into the streets without warning or explanation.

My parents, who had devoted decades of honest work to the system, also found themselves without the pensions they had so carefully planned for. It took years before they finally began receiving payments, but by then, inflation had reduced their value to mere pennies, barely enough to buy bread.

I couldn't help but ask them: How right did you teach me to follow in your footsteps? What did those steps ultimately achieve? Their belief in the supposed stability of the economic and political system turned out to be nothing more than an illusion, one that left countless people disillusioned and hollow.

You've likely heard it often: "That person drives a Mercedes and owns a massive villa, but ordinary people like us shouldn't even dream of such things." They call you, and still call you, "ordinary mortals," as if certain things are "not meant for you." But who exactly are they meant for if we are all mortal?

This world is overflowing with abundance; indeed, a piece of it can become yours if you truly desire it. If beautiful homes exist, who says one of them can't be yours? If there are countless foreign countries to explore, who says you won't walk their streets one day? If luxury cars like Mercedes exist, where is it written that you can't own one?

No one, anywhere, anytime, can guarantee you'll achieve everything you desire. But by the same token, no one can ensure you won't. If there are no guarantees against it, you can have everything you set your heart on if you truly want it.

Another harmful myth drilled into us is the phrase: "It's not harmful to want," always followed by a discouraging "but..." Yet the truth is, it isn't harmful to want. Wanting is essential. You must like it! You must be sincere in your wants and desires—because only through genuine desire do dreams take shape and become reality.

***

One day, I came across a photograph of an old, crumbling two-story house at the foot of a towering mountain, slowly encroaching upon the structure and the surrounding land. A landslide or mudflow could wipe out the house at any moment, even in fair weather. The image was deeply unsettling, especially knowing it was a residential home where several families lived. Indeed, there were children among them, too.

Reactions to the photograph varied, but most saw it as a grim depiction of harsh reality. Everyone understood that the house would be gone sooner or later, whether from inevitable collapse or the merciless forces of nature. And what about the people? Some might escape; others might not. But even if they survived, they would lose their home, a place they called their foundation of stability.

But is there no way out? There is probably more than one. In such a situation, I would have found a way to escape. Those who accept living under the constant shadow of impending disaster will remain. But those who understand that every person has the freedom to choose, move, and shape their future will find a way to change their circumstances and avoid unnecessary risks. The power of choice is a beacon of hope in the darkest times.

Society perpetuates countless myths through television screens, newspapers, and magazines, dividing people into winners and losers. I often hear people say that I'm lucky that everything in my life goes smoothly because I am fortunate.

But first, my life has had its fair share of failures and real, painful setbacks. If I were to recount only those moments, some might feel comforted, as parts of my life could easily be mistaken for a kind of personal hell.

Secondly, we assign ourselves the roles of "winner" or "loser." Many people find comfort in playing the role of a victim, as in today's society, victims tend to receive more positive attention. Criticizing or raising your voice against a victim is seen as cruel, and it's considered inappropriate to add to their suffering. But in many cases, playing the victim is just a disguise, a convenient mask to maintain the illusion of stability and avoid confronting deeper truths.

I've known a married couple for over twenty years. Their marriage wasn't built on love; the woman, at 18, was afraid of becoming an old maid (a fear shaped by the societal norms of the time) and decided to marry at the first opportunity. The weight of societal expectations was a heavy burden on her young shoulders. From the very beginning, their relationship was plagued by arguments and conflict. The birth of their son, yet another concession to the traditional belief that every family, no matter how troubled, must have children, only added to their challenges. Although the wife resented her husband, and the feeling was mutual, neither tried to improve their situation.

Over time, the husband slipped into alcoholism, while the wife, burdened with guilt and frustration, sought comfort in an affair with a married lover. She became the primary breadwinner as her husband squandered his entire salary on alcohol. The constant stress took a serious toll on her health, leaving her emotionally and physically drained, a state that was a direct result of her circumstances.

When we met occasionally, her conversations revolved around endless complaints about her unhappy life, how exhausted and trapped she felt, and how, at times, she wished it could all end. I once asked her, "Why don't you get a divorce?" Assuming the child might be the reason, I was surprised to learn that the boy rarely even saw his father, who was often away drinking.

Her reasons differed: She'd have to give up half of the one-bedroom apartment and the furniture and other belongings they'd accumulated over the years. Knowing he'd likely waste it all, the thought of handing over that "wealth" to her husband was too much for her to bear.

Some time passed. The son grew up and fell in with the wrong crowd, having lacked the positive influence of a father, while his mother remained preoccupied with earning a living. She now had a three-room apartment instead of the original one-bedroom, but the same alcoholic husband—and the same old complaints. For years, she said, she had ceased to feel like a wife or even a woman, living instead as a mere shadow, a workhorse. I asked her:

"You've spent the last twenty years proving to yourself that you can survive without your husband's salary, right?"

"Yes! Everything you see here, I bought with my own money," she answered proudly. "He had nothing to do with it! He's still drinking away every paycheck, just like he always has. I've had enough of it!" Her resilience in the face of adversity was truly inspiring. "But he's still living with you under the same roof. Previously, you had reasons for postponing divorce, such as your son or the one-bedroom apartment. But what's stopping you now?"

"But he's still living with you under the same roof. Previously, you had reasons for postponing divorce — your son or the one-bedroom apartment. But what's stopping you now?"

"Because I'd have to split this apartment in half, and I'm no fool! I earned it with my own hands. I won't give up a thing! What if he brings some new woman to enjoy everything I worked for? No way! I'd rather keep living like this. Everyone else lives this way; I'm not the first, and I won't be the last. But I'm not about to lose what I earned through my blood, sweat, and tears."

***

"You're not the first, and you won't be the last" words that feel like blows to the head, a form of subtle programming that I, too, had to endure. When I failed to get accepted into medical school on my first attempt, despite answering every question correctly, I was convinced that a mistake had been made. However, in the final chemistry exam, I was deliberately given a grade of three (satisfactory) to ensure my average score wouldn't exceed the required passing threshold.

At that time, I was oblivious that university admissions were merely a numbers game, a bureaucratic exercise where rules were twisted to fit a set quota of students, many of whom were admitted through personal connections, regardless of merit. I appealed because I couldn't accept the unjust downgrading of my score on the last exam. However, challenging the exam board's decision was like challenging the institution's political structure. The head of the appeals committee and its members were all drawn from the university's party committee, an apparent conflict of interest.

I entered the room, where a few people sat at tables, their faces marked by sour, disapproving expressions. I greeted them politely, hoping for acknowledgment, but no one smiled. The head of the committee, who also led the institute's party committee, leaned forward and asked in a cold, iron tone:

"Well, what exactly do you disagree with?"

Despite the intimidating atmosphere, I took a breath and tried to maintain my composure. "I completed all the tasks," I said. "I even solved the problem in two different ways. I know I made no mistakes; chemistry is one of my favorite subjects. I even competed in the Olympiads..."

The head's expression hardened, and he interrupted me harshly. "Did anyone ask you to solve the problem in two ways? That's where you went wrong!"

His words hit me like a slap in the face. I blinked, struggling to stay calm. "But why does it matter how many ways I solved it? The result is still the same - it's correct."

His scowl deepened, and he snapped, "Enough with your complaints! You're not the first, and you won't be the last! Everyone wants to get into medical school, but not all doors are open. Understand?"

At that moment, I felt a painful truth settle in my chest: knowledge alone doesn't open every door, especially those guarded by systems built on rot. This 'rot' was nepotism, favoritism, and disregard for merit that plagued the system. And like a swamp that has been festering for centuries, these systems endure, whether we like it or not.

Then, I realized how deeply flawed my father's beliefs had been. He had always told me, "If you study well in school and excel at university, you'll be needed by someone, by something, and a bright future will surely await you." But now I knew that wasn't true. Success didn't depend on how much knowledge you had or how well you mastered it. It hinged on how you applied that knowledge and whether you could find or create the conditions to use it.

Sadly, most people seem to program their minds with negative dogmas that suppress their will rather than nurturing positive thoughts that spark creativity and foster growth. These 'negative dogmas' are the beliefs that success is only for the privileged, that merit is not always rewarded, and that the system is inherently unfair. Without those positive ideas, people remain trapped, unable to thrive or succeed in any field they choose.

***

Let's return to the concept of stability. The belief in and search for stability is another myth, a comforting illusion that dulls human consciousness, gradually turning people into zombies of rigid systems.

If we consider the laws of physics, in a closed system, the universal law of energy conservation states that the total amount of energy remains constant; it doesn't disappear but merely shifts from one form to another. In this sense, such a system could be called "stable." Yet even here, energy is always in motion. However, perfectly isolated systems don't exist and never will. We live in open systems, meaning our world is constantly interacting with external forces and undergoing change.

The human body is also an open system. It requires food intake, energy generation and utilization, and waste elimination. But just as the body never fully absorbs all the nutrients it consumes, our consciousness also needs "food," information that we process but never fully absorb. While our mind feeds on information, it also influences our choices, what we eat, how we act, and how we feel. It governs our words, emotions, and behavior.

Interestingly, some wealthy people have even embraced a strange trend called "dumpster diving," the free movement. This movement, particularly popular in New York and across Europe, involves people gathering to search through public dumpsters, scavenging for discarded food. Freegans take pride in finding alternative ways to meet their needs, not just for food but also for housing and clothing, believing that they are rejecting the wastefulness of consumer culture. This rejection of consumer culture can be seen as a form of liberation, freeing individuals from the constraints of materialism and fostering a sense of independence.

Surprisingly, "elite" dumpsters exist even in some European capitals, where some consider discarded goods luxurious. People make This conscious choice, though I doubt many of you would willingly embrace such a lifestyle.

In the end, the search for stability becomes a misleading pursuit. Systems, whether biological or social, are in constant flux. Knowledge and awareness allow us to adapt to these changing conditions, but clinging to the myth of stability only hinders growth. As many seek it, stability doesn't exist; it's the illusion of permanence within an ever-changing reality. Embracing this reality can be empowering, as it opens up a world of possibilities and potential for growth.

The pursuit of stability is a societal illusion, a comforting bluff. You must abandon this illusion if you genuinely want to improve your life. No successful entrepreneur ever began their journey by seeking stability. On the contrary, many of them walked away from secure jobs with modest, predictable salaries. They were trapped within four walls, surrounded by coworkers who, despite resenting their monotonous routines, were content to settle for the illusion of "stability." Actual progress demands stepping out of that comfort zone and embracing uncertainty. This requires courage and determination, but the rewards can be immense.

***

Another widely accepted illusion is the myth of responsibility, which often fuels the 'endless game of victims and heroes. 'We are responsible for those we have tamed,' goes the phrase, a belief deeply ingrained in our societal norms. It's a belief that we are duty-bound to those we have influenced or 'tamed. ' It often justifies unkind actions towards those we haven't 'tamed' or couldn't 'tame' but whom we still use to our advantage.

It's worth noting that these words aren't some ancient folk wisdoms. They belong to Antoine de Saint-Exupéry, the author of The Little Prince. Responsibility, as a concept, is something we've invented for ourselves. Often, it feels like a burden, a debt. And who enjoys being in debt? No one. That's why responsibility is frequently experienced as something forced to be fulfilled against one's will.

Humanity has invented countless obligations toward people, things, and ideas, creating an endless game of victims and heroes. This game, a product of our societal constructions, often places individuals in the roles of either the victim, burdened with responsibilities, or the hero, who takes on these responsibilities. But does the birth of a child automatically impose duties on the mother? I don't think so. What happens is that her life changes profoundly; her existence now intersects with the

109

child's life. How deeply they connect, however, is a deeply personal matter between the two of them.

For example, a mother could force-feed her child with frustration, saying, "I am your mother, so I have to feed you. Stop spitting out your porridge!" Or, with a smile, she could calmly explain, "Without food, people can get sick or even die." In the second case, feeding the child is no longer burdensome; it becomes a natural, compassionate act.

Which is better: terminating a pregnancy or abandoning a child after birth?

In modern society, abortion is often seen as an acceptable solution because it spares individuals the "burden" of parenting responsibilities. By choosing not to carry the pregnancy to term, both the woman and especially the man are freed from the need to alter their lives for the sake of the child.

However, if a woman chooses not to have an abortion, carries the child to term, and then leaves the baby at the hospital, society labels her as irresponsible. Some self-proclaimed defenders of morality are quick to condemn her, eager to strip her of parental rights and punish her so harshly that she might never again want to bear children.

The lives of abandoned children follow many paths. Some are adopted into loving and stable families, enjoying the kind of life every child deserves. At the same time, in another seemingly "successful" family, one that lacks nothing except love and peace, a child might suffer from violence and neglect. Meanwhile, in a home ravaged by alcoholism, another child struggles for survival, deprived of food, warmth, clothing, and the care they need.

So, where do duties and responsibilities indeed lie? Whose responsibility is it to care, and what are the limits of that responsibility? How often does society challenge the powerful and wealthy, those who financially sustain society yet neglect their own families?

Laws exist for those who break them, and obligations are imposed on those who ignore them. Responsibility often serves as a mask for irresponsibility. The more we try to justify ourselves, the deeper we become entangled in the endless game of "Victim and Hero."

**

Some readers might protest after reading this: If responsibility and obligation are merely human-made concepts, won't that encourage people to stop fulfilling their duties and act irresponsibly in their words and deeds?

Curious, I asked the Angel to explain why obligations exist only for those who fail to fulfill them.

The Angel responded gently: "Look closely at the natural world around you, of which you are also a part. When a fish lays its eggs, is it obligated to care for its offspring?"

I thought for a moment. "I don't think the idea of obligation applies to fish."

The Angel nodded. "And what about a dog? Is a dog obligated to care for its puppies?"

"No, it's not," I answered. "Some animals nurture their youth, while others don't; that's how nature works. But these behaviors aren't obligations."

The Angel smiled. "And no one accuses animals that leave their offspring to survive on their own of neglecting their responsibilities or being irresponsible, do they?"

"That's true," I agreed.

The Angel leaned closer. "And why is that?"

I thought again. "Perhaps because humans believe animals are intellectually inferior and lack emotions or feelings."

The Angel's eyes twinkled with understanding. "But that's not true. Animals experience emotions and feelings, though these may not fit neatly within human definitions."

After a brief pause, the Angel continued: "Now, let's return to the concept of obligations. At their core, obligations are rules, demands, and laws crafted by society to control some people through others to enforce submission. Reminders of obligations are reminders of the social framework within which people are expected to operate. But does everyone follow these rules? Does everyone fulfill their duties?"

"Not everyone. But does that mean parents aren't obligated to fulfill their parental duties or care for their newborn child?"

The Angel responded gently: "No one owes anything to anyone because everyone is born free of obligations and leaves this world with nothing, not even their responsibilities. *Caring for a child is not a duty but an expression of care.* It is an act of love. If parents feel no love or care for their child, the child will only receive what the parents are willing to give. From the outside, such a family might appear to be the perfect parental responsibility model, fulfilling all expected duties. But inside, that family can feel like a prison, especially for those with no means or opportunity to escape its confines."

"So, are parents not obligated to care for their children?"

The Angel gave a knowing smile. "If you are forced to do something against your will, how long will you have the patience to keep doing it? And what kind of person will you become after enduring suppression and humiliation? Will you feel any joy or pride from fulfilling those duties if, in the process, you grow to resent both those who forced you and those for whom you performed those tasks?"

The Angel's voice softened. "When people truly want to care, they will. When people genuinely want to love, they will. Love and care expressed through actions rather than empty words naturally erase the need for reminders of forced obligations. In true care, there is no place for coercion; it flows freely from the heart."

"What about workplace obligations toward employers or employees?" I asked the Angel.

The Angel responded: "No one is obligated to offer someone a job or provide them with a livelihood. Some people earn their bread by exchanging their labor for the products of others, building reserves that can be shared or saved for the future. Others willingly accept modest wages, leaving most of the profit to those who provide the working conditions and teach them how to meet expectations.

An employer is not required to pay wages out of obligation; it is an act of care, a return of value to those who contribute through their labor. Likewise, no worker is forced to labor for anyone; they choose, of their own free will, to exchange their work for the wage offered by the employer. Workers can leave anytime, just as employers can release them from their duties.

The laws designed to protect the rights of employers and employees are merely reminders for those who would break them. For those who respect these rules, such laws are unnecessary. Love and care do not require obligations or responsibilities, they arise naturally, without coercion."

I paused, contemplating the Angel's words. Can love and care genuinely exist under compulsion, born out of obligation or responsibility toward someone? If a light shines brightly in a room, what sense is there in blindfolding those inside, preventing them from using it?

Similarly, when love and care are given out of duty, they cease to be genuine; they become hollow gestures, part of a game driven by fear of judgment. Beneath such acts lies an anxious thought: 'What will others say?'

***

"It's time we talked about fear," I said, settling comfortably into a soft leather armchair in the cozy library at home. The Angel sat beside me in an identical chair, his expression calm and attentive.

"I think we should talk about thoughts first," the Angel suggested.

"Or perhaps about words?" I offered.

The Angel smiled. "Let's start with words since thoughts are formed from words, not just words." He paused and then added, "You can be the teacher, and I'll take the role of the student."

I knew the Angel had already grasped the essence of everything, while I had only begun to scratch the surface of the universe's knowledge. I couldn't truly teach him anything. Still, I valued his wisdom. It recalled a quote I'd read recently: "To become a great teacher, you must teach others while continuing to learn yourself."

Words are not mere labels for objects, emotions, or phenomena. They carry a profound meaning shaped over millennia by civilizations. A word is a symphony of letters, and its sound produces vibrations, a concept deeply rooted in physics.

The Angel nodded in agreement. "Indeed, words resonate."

"Both literally and figuratively," I added.

The Angel's expression softened. "Let's leave aside the figurative meaning for now. Everything has a literal meaning, but people perceive it in their way. Every word carries a personal meaning for each individual."

"And from these personal meanings, collective meaning can emerge," I concluded.

"Let's get back to the physics of words," the Angel said.

"Sound is the vibration of particles," I explained. "In essence, it's oscillation. Particles or objects - can be anything. But sound isn't just vibration caused by the collision of two objects."

The Angel nodded. "In analog equipment, sound is represented by fluctuations of electrical current in a circuit, known as analog signals. Digital equipment still relies on electrical signals, but sound waves are converted into discrete numerical data called samples. This data is processed as digital signals and later converted into analog signals by a digital-to-analog converter for playback through speakers or headphones. While digital systems don't transmit continuous analog waves directly, they still rely on electrical impulses to process and reproduce sound."

"Exactly," I agreed. "But sound interacts with every object it touches, including the human body, especially the nerve endings in our auditory system. The signal travels to the brain, where it's processed. This is one channel through which sound reaches the brain's cells. The brain engages in a more complex process regarding words, not just simple sounds. It decodes the sound waves, and the meaning embedded within them."

The Angel leaned forward, intrigued. "What other channels do sound use to transmit itself?"

I continued: "Through vibration itself. Every cell in our body, down to the smallest particle, vibrates when exposed to sound. Our bodies act both as conductors and absorbers of these vibrations. For example, bone tissue is an excellent resonator.

This interaction between sound and the body follows the principles of sound physics. The takeaway is simple: the oscillations produced by sound, including those from spoken words, directly affect the human body through the vibrations they generate."

The Angel's warm smile conveyed his agreement with our shared understanding. "Agree!"

"In ancient times, it was said that words had the power to kill. The priests of ancient Egypt possessed the knowledge of the word. Were there other civilizations that mastered this science?"

"Yes, they were," the Angel replied.

"The civilizations of ancient India. According to their teachings, specific sound combinations could influence the brain and the body, inducing various states of mind. Some sound patterns were believed to disrupt brain function and even cause death. Because of the potential danger, this knowledge was kept strictly secret, accessible only to a select group of priests.

Modern research has confirmed that sounds with different rhythms and, therefore, different oscillations affect brain cells uniquely. This is primarily by influencing their electrical activity, which is essential for the body's functioning. Sound can trigger aggression, induce calm, lull someone to sleep, or inspire and uplift their mood.

Some words or sound combinations were forbidden, while others have survived. For example, words like 'hallelujah' and 'om.' While their original meanings may have been lost, the vibrations produced when these words are spoken create oscillations that calm the mind. Many sounds positively affecting the brain and the body have become integral to Eastern religions and meditation practices."

"Now, let's move from the physics of sound to another kind of physics," the Angel said, guiding my thoughts in the right direction.

"Every word carries meaning, not just a combination of sounds. When a word is spoken, it's perceived one way; when it's read, it's perceived differently. Depending on the emotional tone conveyed through speech or writing, the meaning may remain or shift. Yet, every word holds energy, not just the energy of sound vibrations, since silent reading produces no sound, but the energy inherent in the word's meaning."

"This brings us to the nature of thought, an arrangement of words in a specific order that creates a meaning greater than the sum of the individual words."

"And here we arrive at the concept of the energy of thought," I agreed. "The transmission of this energy functions through vibrations, governed not only by the principles of applied physics but also by the more profound laws of the universe.

The human brain acts as a receiver of signals, yet it often can't tell whether the signal comes from within, through consciousness, imagination, the subconscious, or from the outside world. For example, athletes were asked to imagine running a race while remaining perfectly still. When scientists measured their brain activity, the areas responsible for controlling the leg muscles were activated as if the athletes were physically running."

I paused, reflecting. "Many other experiments have demonstrated that thoughts not only influence a person's emotional state but also impact the functioning of cells within the body. Unfortunately, many people dismiss these findings as unscientific, remaining skeptical of anything that can't be neatly explained through the laws of physics, chemistry, or mathematics."

"You've probably noticed that science worldwide is shifting toward accepting things that seemed unbelievable or impossible a hundred years ago."

I nodded in agreement.

"When I first tried to share my understanding of the world and explained that my knowledge is part of universal knowledge, not merely a product of my imagination, many people didn't want to hear it. Some thought something was wrong with me, believing that someone as educated as I couldn't say such 'nonsense.' But now, these ideas are being discussed openly in books and on television and are received in a completely different light.

More and more people are embracing these concepts, and their followers are multiplying. Where once people were afraid to listen to me, now I receive calls from those working in similar fields. A network of like-minded individuals is forming, not just isolated dots scattered across the globe but also people establishing real, meaningful connections. And there's a reason for this, isn't there?"

"Exactly," the Angel replied. "You've probably heard some people say that human civilization might destroy itself through reckless behavior toward the environment. But that's not the real reason we seek to connect people into a network, as you aptly put it. What you are witnessing is the emergence of a new kind of human being or, more precisely, the birth of a new civilization capable of moving across different informational and energetic levels. If this idea seems absurd now, it's only because humanity has drawn too rigid a line between matter, consciousness, information, and energy."

"With environmental disasters, reckless energy consumption, and political intrigues that could, at any moment, lead to the use of weapons of mass destruction, it feels like human civilization and our planet are steadily approaching the brink of self-destruction," I said.

The Angel responded:

"Energy exists in limitless abundance everywhere - you must learn how to harness it. It is humanity itself that hinders the adoption of new energy sources. Environmental problems can be resolved with thoughtful, informed approaches. To eliminate political intrigues, you need a generation of thinkers who deeply understand the interconnected nature of matter, energy, and information. This change will come, but not overnight. It is a creative process that requires time from your earthly perspective. There will be no apocalypse, not from our point of view."

***

After a brief break, I delved back into the profound influence of words on the human brain, behavior, emotions, and feelings. The particular aspect that piqued my interest was the impact of names, given that individuals hear their names more frequently than any other word. This is especially intriguing for those deeply interested in psychology, philosophy, and the interplay between language and identity. Most interactions begin with someone addressing the individual by name, often emphasizing it to ensure the person knows they are being spoken to.

As we all know, parents and relatives call children by their names from birth, hoping to capture the baby's attention. But can the choice of a name influence a person's character, personality, or even chances of success in life? As a community interested in psychology, philosophy, and the interplay between language and identity, we can explore this question together.

To satisfy our shared curiosity, I compiled a list of people and grouped them by the sound of their names, not their formal names (often long and seldom used in daily life) but the shorter versions people most commonly use. For example, my official name in Russian is Elena, and in Ukrainian, Olena, but my family and friends usually call me Lena. This is a journey of exploration that we can all embark on together.

After grouping individuals with the same names, I searched for shared personality traits and, where possible, analyzed both their past and present. Even brief encounters or casual conversations create a connection that allows us to observe aspects of a person's life, offering insights into their temperament, behavior, and inner world.

Interestingly, I found many commonalities among people with the same names. Even their behavior revealed unexpected similarities.

I asked the Angel how much a person's name influences them.

"A name alone cannot define a person's character or guarantee their future," the Angel began. "However, it plays an important role because it is one of the sounds people hear most often, especially in childhood, when identity is still forming. A name becomes a powerful signal, a sound imbued with meaning, and meaning carries energy."

"Imagine yourself sitting in the center of a crowded square," the Angel continued. "You remain still, but all around you, the world shifts constantly. The sky and clouds change, the wind picks up or calms, leaves fall from trees, and the faces of passersby come and go. Birds and flies fly by, and sounds swirl around you in an endless flow. Everything is in motion. Even though you sit still, every sight, sound, and breath of air touches you, leaving subtle imprints. In that moment, you are like an antenna, receiving signals from your surroundings."

"So, does this mean a person's name has limited influence on their personality?" I asked.

"Not at all," the Angel replied. "Names are deeply significant. They carry sound and meaning, and a person hearing their name so often, especially in childhood, can shape their emotional world. But your name is only one part of the symphony of sounds your experience. Words, thoughts, and the environment around you also play a role in your development."

I reflected aloud. "There are traditions among certain cultures where newborns are named after objects, phenomena, or animals. Parents believe naming their children after these things will impart desirable qualities."

"In a way, that is true," the Angel replied. "The name becomes a kind of aspiration, a seed planted with hope. Some parents name their daughters after delicate flowers like Lotus and their sons after strong objects like Stone. This isn't just poetic; it sets intentions for the child's future."

"So, it's a form of programming?" I asked.

"You could see it that way," the Angel agreed. "A name offers a framework, a starting point. But it doesn't determine everything. Much like planting a seed, the environment in which the child grows, relationships, experiences, and personal choices will ultimately shape the outcome."

For instance, 'Elena' means 'chosen one,' 'Peter' translates to 'stone,' and 'Alexander' means 'defender of people.' Yet many parents choose names based on their sounds without knowing their deeper meanings. This lack of awareness doesn't diminish the potential influence of these names. They can still shape a person's identity and aspirations, even if the individual is unaware of the name's original meaning.

"That is why it's important to be mindful when choosing names," the Angel advised. "Words carry weight, and a name is more than a label; it's part of the identity a person grows into. However, it is unwise to attribute a person's behavior solely to their name. A name can shape, but it does not dictate."

I thought momentarily, then said, "Recently, I read about how words, thoughts, and sounds affect the brain. It suggested that vibrations might explain their influence, though the concept remains unproven."

"You are on the right path," the Angel responded. "All things - thoughts, words, even emotions - create vibrations. Although science has not yet measured every aspect of these effects, it will. What is certain is that energy never disappears; it transforms."

Energy takes many forms: kinetic, potential, thermal, electromagnetic, etc. But there are still forms of energy humanity has yet to understand fully. For now, we call them the energy of thought, the energy of consciousness, and the energy of the psyche. These forms of energy are not yet fully understood by science, but they are believed to play a significant role in shaping our experiences and interactions.

"Let's talk about Dr. Masaru Emoto's research," I suggested. "He claimed that water responds to words, sounds, and thoughts by changing its crystalline structure. He exposed water to different sounds, prayers, and intentions. When the water was frozen, the crystals formed were either symmetrical and beautiful, or distorted and irregular, depending on the energy they had absorbed."

While Emoto's work is fascinating, it remains controversial in many ways. His experiments lacked the controls and objectivity required by modern science. However, the idea that energy, whether thought or sound, can influence matter is not far-fetched. Suppose we consider the implications of Emoto's research. In that case, it suggests that our thoughts and words can affect the world around us, even if we can't fully understand or measure this influence yet.

"If everything is connected by energy," I asked, "why not reveal all the universe's secrets to us? Why not tell us exactly how life began or how everything came into existence?"

The Angel smiled. "That is a very human question," he said. "But think of it this way: if I gave you a tank of wine and told you to drink it all at once, could you manage? Even if you could, what joy would be left in discovery?"

I laughed at the image of myself beside a giant tank of wine.

"There are no secrets," the Angel continued. "Everything is open to you because you are part of the universe you study. But understanding takes time, and knowledge must come in stages. If you are given too much too soon, it becomes overwhelming."

"Are you worried that humanity might destroy itself?" I asked.

"We are not here to destroy you," the Angel replied gently. "For God, there are no monsters. All beings are His creation, and all are loved. Creation is not about violent endings but salvation and renewal."

"But humanity could still destroy itself?" I pressed.

"Yes," the Angel said softly. "You have the power to do that without our help. But you also have the power to create, heal, and transform. You are beautiful; I'll repeat it."

It was getting late, and I had other matters to attend to, so we decided to pause our conversation.

Speaking with the Angel is always possible, but beyond these conversations, there is also the surrounding world and work to engage with.

***

We returned once again to the topic of how words affect us. Words form the foundation of our thoughts, and how we combine them can have an even more profound impact than individual words alone. Since our consciousness acts as a filter for everything we hear and see, the words of others can directly influence both our mental and physical state.

How we perceive the world around us changes depending on our mood, circumstances, and phase of life. Our interpretation of events shapes what follows. In other words, the creation of our future starts now, with today. If you start your day in a positive frame of mind, your day is more likely to unfold smoothly. This power of positive thinking gives us hope and optimism. However, if you begin the day feeling tired, angry, or frustrated, it's more likely to bring setbacks and challenges. This is how the Law of Attraction works.

Some years ago, I referred to the Law of Attraction as the 'boomerang law' to make its mechanics easier to grasp. Imagine that your thoughts, emotions, and intentions are like the energy you send into the world. This 'energy' is a metaphor for the vibrations you consciously and unconsciously emit through your mindset and feelings. Whether positive or negative, these thoughts become vibrations you radiate. The energy you emit acts like a boomerang: whatever you project will return to you.

This returning energy can manifest itself in various ways. It could come from the emotions of people you encounter, the atmosphere of places you visit, or even subtle, unseen forces shaping your circumstances. For instance, if you're constantly worried about money, you might find yourself in situations reinforcing this worry, such as unexpected bills or financial setbacks. Whether you believe in it or not, this law operates independently of your awareness or desire.

From another perspective, you act as a magnet, attracting the kind of energy you generate most often. If you fill your mind with positive thoughts and emotions, you naturally attract positive experiences. This realization empowers you, as it means you can shape your experiences. But you'll draw more difficulties into your life if your thoughts are dominated by fear, resentment, or negativity.

Try keeping a journal to understand how the Law of Attraction works. Write brief notes daily, recording your thoughts, emotions, and key events. This practice can help you identify the patterns in your thinking and their impact on your experiences.

Here's an example:

You didn't sleep well because your neighbors argued loudly all night, leaving you tired and irritable in the morning. You missed the overcrowded bus and arrived late at work, where your boss was also in a bad mood. Later, you found out your paycheck would be delayed and overheard your colleagues gossiping about others and you.

On your way home, you stopped by the store only to notice that prices had risen again. Your boots got soaked, leaving you cold and shivering. When you arrived home, you discovered the phone had been disconnected because you missed the payment deadline. Your child brought home poor grades, and your spouse stayed late at work celebrating someone's birthday.

By the end of the day, exhausted and frustrated, you lost your temper and yelled at your child. The stress gave you a headache, so you decided to lie down. But heavy thoughts swirled through your mind, making it impossible to relax, and you tossed and turned until morning. When you finally woke up, the headache persisted, and you carried yesterday's exhaustion into the new day.

This example shows how the energy you project creates a cycle of experiences that mirrors your emotional state. When your mind is clouded with frustration, anger, or anxiety, these emotions attract more of the same energy, compounding your difficulties. However, even a tiny shift toward positivity, a moment of patience or gratitude, can change the course of your day, paving the way for better experiences.

The Law of Attraction isn't about pretending to feel good when you don't. It's about becoming aware of your emotional patterns, the recurring feelings and reactions you have in certain situations and gradually shifting them. Begin by noticing how you feel, even in difficult moments. For instance, if you're stuck in traffic, do you feel impatient and frustrated, or do you use the time to listen to your favorite music? If you're facing a challenging task at work, do you feel anxious and overwhelmed, or do you focus on the opportunity to learn and grow? Try redirecting your focus toward something you appreciate, even if it's just a tiny comfort or a fleeting moment of beauty. This isn't about avoiding your problems but changing how you respond to them.

Even small shifts in energy, choosing patience instead of anger or gratitude instead of frustration, can gradually attract better experiences. The boomerang always returns, but you can decide what energy you send out.

Such scenarios, or ones like them, happen to many people almost daily. A vicious cycle forms, making it difficult to see anything joyful or hopeful and even more challenging to break free. However, breaking free from these cycles is possible with self-awareness and a commitment to change. This self-awareness empowers us to take control of our lives. While it's unrealistic to expect anyone to feel happy 24/7, it is possible to maintain a positive outlook and a general sense of satisfaction with life.

The Law of Attraction is simple: if you focus on negativity, you attract more negativity; if you focus on positivity, you attract more positivity. This simplicity should reassure you that you can understand and apply this law. You've probably heard the sayings, "You reap what you sow" or "Money attracts more money." In the same way, joyful thoughts, emotions, and feelings attract more joy and happiness into your life. This simplicity should give you confidence in applying the Law of Attraction.

Negative emotions seem more powerful than positive ones because they carry a more potent, energetic charge. That's why negative experiences can feel overwhelming, and getting stuck in a cycle of frustration, anger, or sadness is easy. But it's important to recognize that you can disrupt that cycle by becoming aware of your thoughts and emotions.

One of the simplest ways to regain emotional balance is to focus on your breath. Many people call this practice meditation, though it requires no special training. Some people tell me they don't know how to meditate because they think it's too complicated. To them, I say, "But you know how to breathe, don't you? Why not start by listening to your breath?"

Find a quiet place in your home where you won't be disturbed for 15 to 20 minutes. Ideally, this spot should be calm and silent. Sit or lie down in a comfortable position, relax your body, and begin breathing naturally.

Don't try to empty your mind or control your thoughts. Just focus on your breath: inhale, exhale, inhale, exhale.

Your breathing will gradually slow down. Don't be alarmed if you start feeling subtle movements or vibrations in your body or head or sense a gentle pulsation within your body. Observe these sensations without judgment. If you feel sleepy, allow yourself to drift into sleep. Your body will take what it needs.

I recommend visualizing a clear blue sky or a beautiful field of flowers to enhance your mood. If you struggle to stop negative thoughts, redirect them toward something joyful or uplifting. The more vivid and joyful your dreams or fantasies are, the more they will help restore your emotional balance.

If you still feel unsure about the impact of your thoughts and emotions, start keeping a journal. Write down your day's events, thoughts, and feelings. Over time, you'll notice patterns of how certain thoughts lead to specific outcomes and how small shifts in your attitude can improve your experiences.

Self-awareness is the first step toward transformation. Once you recognize these patterns, you'll gain the insight to consciously shift your focus and create a life filled with more joy and positivity.

***

Have you ever wondered why some thoughts linger and why words heard in childhood can echo throughout your life? Our minds are shaped by what we think and what others say and do around us. Understanding how words influence a person's life, including yours, reveals that our brain and consciousness are constantly programmed. These programs, whether implanted by others or created by you, determine how the events of your life unfold, your successes or failures, your present, and your future. But remember, you have the power to choose the programs that shape your life.

Consider how often you heard, as a child, that you couldn't have, or even wish for, a particular toy because your parents weren't wealthy. On the one hand, you were taught that wanting something doesn't guarantee you'll get it. But beneath that lesson, a more subtle program was written into your mind: only wealthy people can have what they desire. Since your parents weren't rich, the implication was that neither are you, and therefore, it's pointless to dream of what only the wealthy can afford.

In societies where these ideas take root, dishonesty often becomes normalized to circumvent limitations. This was especially true in the former Soviet Union, where generations learned to take whatever wasn't guarded, no matter how small the opportunity. Ironically, those who stole often found themselves victims of theft, locked in a cycle of dishonesty.

I've witnessed many cases where such behaviors became accepted in daily life. For example, I knew a man who worked as a bus driver on routes between the city and nearby villages. Because the buses were always packed with passengers, drivers could collect fares during the journey to avoid long lines at ticket offices. But passengers rarely receive a ticket. The cash handed over at the door often went straight into the driver's pocket.

The man's wife worked in the cafeteria of a state institution. Every day, she brought home bags of stolen food and groceries. The couple would lay out their "earnings" on the kitchen table before their children in the evenings. Without a word, they programmed their children to believe that stealing and dishonest work were acceptable and preferable to more honest ways of earning a living. And just as with many others, these children likely grew up to follow the same path.

People are quick to notice the faults in others, but they remain blind to their actions. The problem is that negative patterns, once established, reinforce themselves.

Our environment has a powerful influence on us, shaping not only what we do but also how we think and feel. Suppose you listen carefully to the daily news. In that case, you'll notice that most are filled with negativity: reports of military conflicts, rising crime, economic instability, political disputes, diseases, accidents, and natural disasters. A half-hour of news becomes an exhaustive list of everything that went wrong that day. Positive stories are so rare that they seem like anomalies.

What happens to a person constantly exposed to such negativity? What do they feel when they see images of dismembered bodies on TV, watch politicians insult each other or hear angry protestors shouting in the streets? What emotions arise after standing in line for a product, only to encounter an angry, exhausted shop assistant who complains the moment you reach the counter?

Imagine visiting a doctor, only to be met by a frustrated, poorly trained specialist who resents their salary and views you not as a patient needing care but as a walking wallet. Exposure to such experiences accumulates over time. Fear, anger, frustration, humiliation, irritability, and resentment begin to embed themselves in a person's mind like splinters, shaping their perception of the world.

These negative emotions carry a powerful charge of destructive energy. They don't just affect the individual but radiate outward, influencing others and the environment. Negative thoughts and words disturb the delicate balance of a person's life, leading to further problems and setbacks.

Once set in motion, negativity triggers a chain reaction, where one bad event quickly follows another. A person caught in this spiral often finds themselves trapped as difficulties in one area of life spill over into others. Financial struggles create tension in relationships, and health issues arise under the pressure of stress. In turn, illness makes working and earning a living harder, worsening relationships and financial difficulties.

For instance, a sick person becomes an unreliable employee, less valuable to their employer. They struggle to provide for themselves and their family without a steady income, creating another layer of hardship.

The forces that shape our experiences are complex, extending from the smallest interactions in daily life to the vast movements of the universe. It's essential to recognize that negative energy often carries more significant destructive potential than positive energy. Once it accumulates, its impact can be overwhelming and unpredictable. When we harbor negative thoughts and emotions, we radiate that energy outward, and it returns to us with even greater intensity. In essence, we become the architects of our suffering.

This principle is not new; it has been taught by all religions and spiritual traditions and expressed differently but with the same core message: the energy you project will inevitably return to you. The power to change your circumstances lies in your choices about the energy you release into the world. This means that no matter how negative your current situation may seem, there is always the potential for positive change.

Another important factor is how we respond to external energies and influences. While the world around us can profoundly affect us, it is possible to develop a degree of protection against these opposing forces, including the harmful energy of others. Various techniques, practices, and schools offer methods for energetic protection, teaching people how to build resilience against negativity.

However, it's essential to understand that such protection is conditional. It relies on reprogramming the mind and behavior to reduce the impact of negative influences. This process isn't about shutting out the world but about learning to engage with it in a way that maintains emotional equilibrium. Doing so allows you to navigate life's challenges with balance and stability.

It's also essential to avoid isolating yourself in a bubble, cutting yourself off from others to shield yourself. While it may feel safe in the short term, creating artificial barriers can lead to self-destruction. Human beings are inherently social creatures; we thrive in connection with others, and long-term isolation can erode our mental and emotional well-being.

The key lies in balance. People must cultivate harmony within themselves and their relationships with the outside world. Proper protection does not come from withdrawing from life but from learning to stay open to experiences without being overwhelmed.

***

On Christmas Eve, our friends from Buffalo invited my husband and me to visit. We had the pleasure of meeting an intriguing man named Mark. We gathered in a cozy corner of the clinic. We immersed ourselves in a conversation that becomes more relevant with each passing day: the interplay between energy and matter, consciousness and material reality. This topic continues to fascinate many.

The seven of us, adults of various ages, backgrounds, and professions, engaged in a lively discussion about how the Law of Attraction unfolds in our lives. It was a month filled with encounters that either validated long-held ideas or confirmed insights brewing for years, sparking a sense of wonder and curiosity in our exploration of this powerful force.

Our conversation began with the recently premiered film The Secret, which had already sparked profound shifts in thinking for many viewers. While the film followed the familiar Hollywood formula, with vibrant lighting, dramatic sound effects, and fast-paced scenes, it effectively conveyed a powerful message about the workings of the Law of Attraction. This dynamic presentation allowed it to reach a broad and diverse audience, regardless of their backgrounds or belief systems.

Interestingly, an acquaintance had given me a copy of "The Secret" just as I was working on this book and reading "Ask and It Is Given" by Esther and Jerry Hicks. My conversations with the Angel often mirrored those between Esther and Abraham, who answered her questions in much the same way the Angel responded to mine. By design, I was later invited to meet Esther in Toronto, deepening my understanding of these teachings. Over the past few months, the books on the Law of Attraction by Esther and Jerry Hicks have sparked countless discussions, including the lively one we were having that evening.

Another book that beautifully bridges the gap between science and spirituality is "The Field" by Lynne McTaggart. McTaggart embarked on an extraordinary journey, traveling across multiple countries to meet leading experts in quantum physics, mathematics, biochemistry, and other disciplines. They all strived to uncover the laws that govern the universe, from the smallest particles to the vastness of the cosmos.

In "The Field," McTaggart synthesizes modern scientific knowledge about the universe's structure and the laws governing the energy of vibrating electrons and subatomic particles. Her work demonstrates that we are all part of a unified energy field, expressing and manifesting this energy subtly and physically.

What struck me most was how closely McTaggart's findings aligned with the insights I had received from the Angel and the knowledge Abraham shared with Esther. This remarkable synchronicity reaffirmed that truth flows through many channels, scientific, spiritual, and intuitive, and ultimately converges at the same essential understanding.

As I mentioned earlier, the Angel is not a singular entity. It is not a collection of distinct beings, nor are these entities' beings' in the conventional sense. Instead, they are complex manifestations of energy and information. Similarly, Abraham, who communicates with Esther, presents himself in the plural, not as a singular being but as a non-physical source of knowledge and energy. When the Angel manifests as a singular presence, it facilitates communication, making our interaction more manageable for me to comprehend. Likewise, though Abraham refers to himself in the plural or as 'They,' he takes on a masculine identity and is often perceived as 'He.'

During our Christmas Eve gathering, the conversation turned toward sharing knowledge about the energetic changes in the universe. Just a few years ago, I would have hesitated to discuss such topics with people I didn't know, fearing I might be dismissed as "crazy" or "delusional."

Yet, the people I meet and engage with on these topics come from all over the world, with diverse educational backgrounds and life experiences. Many are my age, speak different languages, and follow various traditions. And yet, we all seem to receive information from a shared Source that goes by many names: God, Angels, the Bio-Informational Field, the Bio-Energetic Field, the Holy Spirit, Abraham, Egregore, and more. This unity in diversity strengthens our shared journey and reassures us that we are not alone.

Many of us have likely pondered the question: What would happen if these encounters were not coincidences? And if more people are experiencing an awakening of consciousness, does this suggest that higher forces are intervening in our lives in response to some threat to humanity?

The Angel's answer came without hesitation, bringing comfort and peace: There is no threat despite the environmental crises, resource depletion, and other challenges facing us. According to the Angel, the universe holds infinite sources of energy. The real challenge lies in learning to access these sources wisely while minimizing the harm caused by our continued reliance on traditional fuels.

We must also recognize that we live in an information age, where knowledge can be exchanged instantly through high-speed communication networks. This allows people to find like-minded souls and connect across vast distances, accelerating the awakening of consciousness and creating a ripple effect across the globe.

***

I asked the Angel if the individuals who seemed to connect with the informational energy field were specially chosen. The answer was yes: the universe selects specific individuals to serve as messengers of its knowledge. But what criteria determine this selection?

There are many criteria, but the most essential is the willingness and ability to apply the knowledge received. To access higher knowledge, one must become like a child, free from worldly distractions, open to learning, and receptive to new insights. If you observe the behavior of a healthy child, you'll notice that they live fully in the present moment, embracing each experience with joy and curiosity. A child accepts what is given without resistance and finds happiness in the simplest things.

At birth, a child knows nothing of language or worldly knowledge; their life is a discovery process, a universe waiting to be explored. Just as children open themselves to the world, it opens itself in return. In the same way, to receive the universe's knowledge, we must remain open and unresisting. Sometimes, the answers you receive are not what you expect or desire. In my own experience, there have been moments when the answers from above disappointed or even shocked me. However, I learned that these truths were necessary for my growth and that accepting them required setting aside my ego.

Openness, however, is not enough. The ability to receive knowledge also demands humility, the ability to silence the ego, and the ability to listen deeply. Many people unconsciously create their answers, fixed patterns, or templates and, in doing so, close themselves off to genuine insight. When answers don't align with their expectations or desires, they stop listening, only hearing what they wish to hear.

Another essential criterion is the absence of fear when engaging with the unknown and the ability to respect all that exists, even if current scientific laws cannot explain it. I have often encountered frustration or anger from people who do not believe in God. What many fail to realize is that atheism, too, is a belief system, a faith in the absence of God. Interestingly, when you speak with such individuals about the structure and laws of the universe without invoking the word "God," it often becomes clear that they believe in an underlying informational energy field that connects all things.

While scientific advancements now explain many phenomena, not everyone is familiar with the latest quantum physics, chemistry, and genetics discoveries. These fields are beginning to provide scientific explanations for insights that were once found only in sacred texts. As ancient teachings suggest, "In the beginning, there was Energy." Matter came into existence through light as a manifestation of that energy.

Another vital criterion is the ability to love. Everyone understands Love, but faithful Love goes beyond romantic relationships or physical attraction. It expresses itself in many forms, between parents and children, friends, colleagues, kindred spirits, and even strangers. Love for nature, animals, art, and the environment is another powerful expression of this force. These positive vibrations carry the creative energy of the universe.

I asked the Angel, "What is the most important commandment for us to follow?" After all, we are often taught that our highest duty is to love God. But does God need our Love?

The Angel replied, "The most important commandment is to love yourself. When a person truly loves and respects themselves, that love naturally extends to God, for within every person lies a divine spark, a fragment of the universe. By loving oneself, one can express authentic Love toward others, neighbors, humanity, and the world.

If someone claims to love God but does not love themselves or others, their words are empty. Love that exists only in words is not real Love. Authentic Love reveals itself through actions, both toward oneself and others."

Ultimately, the universe offers its wisdom to those willing to listen, open to learning, and ready to act. The path to growth and fulfillment lies in self-awareness, Love, and honesty, qualities that align us with the flow of universal energy. We can access the universe's profound knowledge only by embodying these traits. This knowledge is not just for personal benefit but for the good of all humanity, creating ripples of positive change that extend far beyond the individual.

The universe chooses those ready to act, not just those seeking knowledge for its own sake. It is not enough to understand spiritual laws intellectually; they must be lived. Change and growth come through action, through the choices we make each day, no matter how small. Love, honesty, openness, and courage are the guiding principles that allow us to move forward in alignment with the universe.

This process has no final destination; it is only continuous learning and evolving. The path unfolds step by step, offering new insights, challenges, and opportunities as we prepare for them. The awakening of consciousness is not a single event but a journey, an ongoing process of becoming more aligned with the truth within us and the world.

When we understand this, we no longer resist the lessons or fear the unknown. Instead, we embrace life as a co-creation with the universe. Every thought and every action sends ripples outward, influencing not just our world but the collective consciousness of humanity.

Ultimately, the universe responds to those who listen, learn, and act. It patiently waits for each of us to align with its flow. As we awaken, we become both students and teachers, messengers of the same truth that echoes through all things: that we are connected, that we are never alone, and that Love is the essence of all creation.

***

There is a wealth of literature on communicating with the 'otherworld', a term that can be interchanged with 'alternative' or 'parallel'. This realm, existing in a different dimension, is intricately connected to our physical world. It is a space where different energies, shaped by their nature and frequency, manifest in various ways.

However, I have always needed to clarify some nuanced concepts - spirits, angels, spiritual teachers, and the Holy Spirit. Through my conversations with the Angel, I understood that these interactions are not with specific individual beings but with an infinite field of energy and information. This field transcends personal identity, lacking the boundaries of singularity or plurality.

This raises an intriguing question: Why do some people encounter unsettling spirits or ghosts while others experience the presence of saints, angels, or the Divine Source? The answer lies within the individual. The energy one connects with reflects one's inner beliefs, inclinations, and openness. Spirits, angels, and teachers manifest energy on different levels, appearing in forms that align with what a person is prepared to receive.

For example, if a person believes in spirits, they will attract communication on that level. If someone seeks the presence of saints, the energy will take on that form, and they may experience visions of the Virgin Mary, Jesus Christ, Saint Peter, or Fatima. Similarly, if a person wishes to connect with a departed relative or a historical figure, they will receive that interaction. In essence, we return to the Law of Attraction: what you seek is what you receive.

There are many theories, assumptions, and speculations about the structure of the otherworld; some suggest that there are hierarchies among spiritual beings or even conflicts between different realms. These theories often arise from the human tendency to investigate the unknown, driven by curiosity.

However, the otherworld operates according to a law of non-interference, also known as the law of respect for free will. This law ensures that no one and nothing will intervene in a person's life unless explicitly invited. Whether someone seeks guidance, assistance, or knowledge, the otherworld only responds when a request is made. This respect for individual autonomy and the right to choose their path instills a sense of security and control.

I have encountered people who were granted access to the "storehouses of knowledge" within the universe. However, many overlooked an essential truth: they are merely guests in a realm that is not theirs.

Imagine you live in an apartment building. Occasionally, you meet neighbors in the elevator; some are friendly, and others are more reserved. One day, your kind neighbors invite you into their home because they enjoy your warmth and friendliness.

As a guest, you enter an unfamiliar space. You don't know how many rooms the apartment has, who else lives there, or what personal stories are hidden behind its walls. Gradually, as you adjust to your surroundings, you become an observer. However, your perspective is limited, and your understanding is incomplete. When you return to your apartment, you might share what you saw and heard. Yet, no matter how objective you try to be, your retelling will inevitably be shaped by your personal interpretation, biases, and experiences.

When a door is open for you, always remember that you remain a guest. This means you will only see a fraction of the whole picture, a small glimpse of another world. As an earthly being, you are not meant to comprehend the entirety of that realm. It is not your place to conclude what happens there. If you encounter something you do not understand, ask the "hosts" directly, but do so without expecting complete answers. Some truths will always remain beyond your reach simply because you are not ready to grasp them fully.

As a guest, approach with humility. Resist the urge to explore every corner out of curiosity. You will be shown only what the hosts decide you are ready to see, no more and no less. Spiritual understanding takes preparation; attempting to grasp it prematurely can do more harm than good. This emphasis on humility fosters a sense of respect and consideration for the spiritual realm.

The most important rule is this: Do not become a gossip. As the Bible warns, if knowledge is entrusted to you from above, it is meant for you alone, and you must safeguard it within yourself. If you need to share what you've learned through conversation or publication, you must first seek permission from the Source. This emphasis on seeking permission fosters a sense of respect and mindfulness in the audience.

Prying into divine matters while ignoring the flaws and "dirt" within your own life is a sign of profound ignorance and disrespect toward the One who created you. Such reckless curiosity carries consequences. After receiving access to higher knowledge, I have known people who lost their gifts, creativity, respect for others, and health. Their lives unraveled, not because they were given this knowledge, but because they allowed the temptation of that knowledge to consume them. They became mere consumers of what was revealed, forgetting the responsibility that accompanies such a gift,

Every word in this book has been written with the permission of the Angel and those who share knowledge with me through various channels. Every moment of my life is filled with deep gratitude to the Angel for the extraordinary gift of creation entrusted to me.

***

People often say one must possess a special gift to connect with other realms. I didn't dwell on whether I had such a divine gift for much of my life. The greatest gift of all is the ability to love, which, in essence, is the ability to create.

Every child is born with the gift of creation. If you observe children closely, you'll notice that they often play alone, inventing their own stories where toys come alive as characters in their private tales. This is not merely imitating the surrounding world but an actual creation. Interestingly, children rarely create evil characters on their own. We, as adults, play a significant role in shaping their perceptions. We introduce them to figures like Baba Yaga, Koschei the Immortal, or wicked dragons. Although many adult-made fairy tales end on a happy note, these sinister figures can leave a lasting impression, planting seeds of fear in a child's mind.

A happy child imagines vibrant, joyful stories with cheerful characters. And if Baba Yaga happens to appear in their story, she often transforms into a kind and benevolent figure. The very notion of fighting evil and destroying villains is something imposed by adults. A child enters this world from a realm where battles and wars do not exist. In that place, energies shift and realigns, but there is no struggle for power or possession.

Every person is born with the gift of creation. Some express it through music, others through art, and many through mastery in their chosen field. However, these gifts must be nurtured, or they risk being forgotten. Too often, people grow up and abandon the idea that they are gifted. But we must remember that these gifts should not be hidden or neglected. They are to be nurtured, to be brought to life. Some prefer to blend into the gray anonymity of the crowd, avoiding the discomfort of standing out. Others slowly stagnate, unwilling to engage in self-improvement or inner growth, becoming consumed by pursuing material wealth and neglecting their spiritual development or substituting it with mere religious formalism.

People can possess multiple gifts. I've often been told I am a "doctor by the grace of God," meaning a naturally gifted healer. Those who have seen my photographs say I have a talent for capturing life's fleeting moments and the beauty of the world around us. Readers of my poetry and prose have commented on my literary gift. My paintings have drawn admiration, with people calling me a gifted artist. I am a skilled speaker and teacher when lecturing at conferences and seminars.

Yet, no matter how often I hear praise for these talents, I know that every gift demands continuous effort, constant refinement, and growth.

Communicating with other realms may or may not require a special gift. It involves being open to receiving information. Many people shield themselves with artificial barriers, cutting themselves off from others and the world. They often expect miracles, an immediate appearance of a spirit, or the instant fulfillment of their desires. When these things don't happen, disappointment is usually expressed in a skeptical dismissal: "This is all nonsense."

However, we all have the potential to act as antennas and transformers for receiving and transmitting energy and information. Some discover this ability by chance, while others need guidance to awaken and develop it.

***

Many psychics refer to themselves as hereditary, claiming the gift of foresight has been passed down through generations. Yet foresight is not embedded in our genes. Instead, these individuals grow up in environments where practices such as clairvoyance, fortune-telling, and magical rituals are encouraged by family members. In other words, hereditary seers and fortune-tellers have mentors, often within their own families, who nurture and develop their gift for prediction.

The gift of foresight is a mysterious ability to connect with the Universal Information Field. Psychics do not perceive a person's life from start to finish, like watching a film. Instead, they receive specific images, like mosaic fragments, that may not always be glimpses of the future or the past. This enigmatic process of obtaining and interpreting these fragments is what makes their abilities so fascinating.

Sylvia Browne, a renowned psychic and author of numerous books, has acknowledged that her predictions are never 100% accurate; her success rate is around 90%. However, this level of precision came through continuous practice and the refinement of her ability to communicate with other realms. For most psychics, prediction accuracy typically falls between 50% and 70%.

157

In truth, we all possess the potential for prediction, even without considering ourselves clairvoyant. On a fundamental level, predicting with 50% accuracy is natural - after all, a prediction either comes true or doesn't.

A few years ago, I had the opportunity to meet a fascinating woman named Lyuda. She was more popular than any doctor or priest in town. A steady stream of people gathered outside her apartment, waiting for their turn to seek her help. I was intrigued by the stories I heard about her, and when a friend decided to visit her, I couldn't resist seeing her in action.

Despite my interest in the supernatural, I've always been cautious around those who claim to be God-gifted psychics, healers, or seers, especially those who promote themselves on television or in newspapers and magazines. Many of them rely more on group hypnosis than on any genuine gift. Some are little more than charlatans, building their reputation through clever advertising and the support of accomplices who skillfully manipulate a trusting audience. This skepticism was the lens through which I viewed my friend's visit to Lyuda.

A friend of mine decided to visit Lyuda, not for healing, but to learn about the future of her relationship with her husband, who, she suspected, might be having an affair. I wasn't thrilled at the thought of sitting for hours in a cramped hallway with other visitors, but I agreed to accompany her, as she was distraught and needed someone by her side.

Lyuda saw her clients in the small entryway of her one-room apartment. When my friend's turn finally came, I intended to wait outside, but Lyuda noticed my friend's distress and kindly invited me to join them. I took a seat in the corner of the room, quietly observing. Her warm invitation and my friend's trust in her created a sense of connection and comfort in the room.

Lyuda sat behind a small table, speaking gently with my friend. Before long, tears welled up in my friend's eyes. The news she received was not what she had hoped for. After a moment, my friend stepped to the other side of the room, and Lyuda began studying her closely, reading her aura, which she said she usually saw as a white light.

I continued watching in silence as Lyuda identified a few health issues affecting my friend. Though her observations were accurate, I wasn't particularly impressed. I already knew about some of these problems, and I couldn't be sure whether my friend had mentioned them during their conversation.

Lyuda never charged money for her sessions. She would say that if people wished to reward her, their offering should reflect their generosity. She preferred not to handle money at all. Instead, visitors would leave cash, food, or occasional gifts on the kitchen table.

As my friend and I were getting ready to leave, Lyuda turned to me and asked,

"Would you like me to take a look at you?"

"I don't mind," I replied, curious to see what methods she used for her clairvoyance and whether she could genuinely read auras.

"Stand in front of me, then," she instructed.

I stepped about two meters away from her and faced her directly. Lyuda began studying me closely.

"This won't do," she said. "Why are you blocking me? Relax, I'm only observing."

She was right. I had instinctively put up a mental protective barrier, preventing her from thoroughly reading my aura and likely more than that. I smiled and allowed the barrier to dissolve, opening myself up to her examination.

Lyuda continued to study me carefully, commenting on the state of various organs, all of which, she noted, appeared perfectly healthy. Then she paused and asked,

"Have you ever had any issues with your spine? A serious injury, perhaps?"

"No," I replied, puzzled. "I've never had any spinal injuries."

Lyuda gave me a long, thoughtful look, her expression contemplative.

"No, I'm certain," she said. "I see a strong distortion in the energy field right here." She stepped closer and pointed to a specific spot on my back where she believed the issue lay. Since I was fully dressed, there was no way she could have seen any scars, deformities, or swelling.

"There was a serious injury at this spot. Let's keep going," she said, stepping back to continue reading.

At the time, I was dealing with a persistent fistula that required urgent surgery, according to medical advice. However, I had decided to delay the procedure for a few weeks, hoping to consult with a more experienced specialist in another city.

"I think we can try to resolve your issue another way," Lyuda suggested. "If it doesn't work, you can still proceed with the surgery."

Her confidence surprised me. No one knew about my condition except me, my husband, and the specialist treating me. It was a profoundly personal issue I hadn't shared with anyone else. Yet Lyuda spoke with quiet certainty, offering her help. Her unexpected insight into my condition challenged my skepticism and left me intrigued.

"All right, I'll come," I said. "How much do I owe you?"

"Nothing," Lyuda replied firmly. "And please, don't leave money on the kitchen table."

I was taken aback. "Why not? Why nothing?"

"Because you are one of the Chosen," she said. "I cannot accept money or any other payment from you. We'll talk about it another time."

Her words left me stunned. What did she mean by "Chosen"? And why was she forbidden from taking payment from me?

When I got home that evening, I started changing clothes and caught a glimpse of my back in the mirror. That's when I saw it, the scar. How could I have forgotten? It was precisely at the spot Lyuda had indicated.

Years earlier, during a course of physical therapy, I had suffered a severe electrical burn. The head of the physiotherapy department was shocked; nothing like it had ever happened under her supervision. One of the electrodes on my lower back had caused a deep burn, penetrating the skin and underlying tissues by about 1.5 centimeters. The wound left behind was the size of a small coin.

When the scab eventually fell off, the hole was large enough to fit the tip of my pinky finger. Along with the physical pain, I began experiencing digestive issues and problems with pelvic organs, as the injury had occurred dangerously close to the lumbar nerve plexus. It took over a year for the wound to heal and for my body to function normally again. The scar faded in time, and I forgot about the ordeal.

Though the burn no longer caused me any significant issues, it had altered the bioenergetic field around my lower spine. That must have been the trauma Lyuda had detected.

***

I began visiting Lyuda almost every day for 20- to 30-minute sessions. She worked with energy, directing and focusing it through her hands. Prayer was an essential part of every session, as Lyuda firmly believed that her gift for healing was a blessing from God.

Her abilities in clairvoyance and healing had emerged after she underwent serious brain surgery. Initially, she resisted the visions that began appearing to her, struggling to make sense of them. She was too afraid to tell her husband about her newfound abilities for a long time. But over time, she accepted her role. Lyuda was an insightful advisor, compassionate listener, and wise teacher. She always insisted that her knowledge and abilities came directly from the Divine.

The sessions soon began to show results. Within a month and a half, the fistula I had been struggling with disappeared. I was overjoyed to feel healthy again. My time with Lyuda reinforced something I had long suspected: that my abilities and insights were connected to the same Source.

Lyuda often encouraged me to pursue healing, reassuring me I had the same potential as hers. In many ways, I was already using my gift. I frequently relied on my intuition to diagnose and treat patients in my medical practice. Women who had struggled with infertility for years conceived within a month or two after my consultations. I could detect malignant tumors at their earliest stages and guide patients, including my father, to seek timely examinations and treatment. These small victories brought joy to my patients and gave me profound personal satisfaction and a sense of hope for the future.

Because of these experiences, I couldn't fully agree with Lyuda's suggestion that I wasn't using my gift. I wasn't publicizing or speaking openly about it, even with those closest to me.

Lyuda also held group prayer sessions for those who believed in God. For others, she healed using light. White light was central to her work; she often incorporated candles into her sessions. What was remarkable was that her knowledge of healing through light and flame seemed instinctive. While modern science can explain the effectiveness of such methods through biophysics, biochemistry, and even quantum physics, Lyuda herself couldn't articulate any scientific rationale. Yet her methods were harmonious, purposeful, and undeniably effective, instilling a sense of reassurance and confidence in those who sought her help.

From Lyuda's apartment window, you could see the domes of a nearby church. During services, she often observed pillars of white energy rising from the church's domes. Her eyes would light up with joy whenever she saw these radiant streams. She believed that these energy streams were a manifestation of God's presence, inspiring her in her healing work.

Most visitors who waited for hours in her cramped hallway weren't seeking healing; they came for fortune-telling. These visitors often came with personal problems and were seeking answers or guidance. But Lyuda didn't particularly enjoy predicting the future. She believed true healing came from within and was not about predicting future events.

"Imagine this," she once told me. "A woman shows up crying, holding a photo of her husband or some object belonging to him. She begs me to find out if he's having an affair, convinced he's cheating. I focus on her, then on her husband, and suddenly, I see the real problem isn't with him but with her. She hasn't been honest, not even with herself. And even if her husband has feelings for someone else, their connection is pure and harmonious. So how am I supposed to tell this bitter, unfaithful wife that the issue lies within her and that I won't help her 'win back' her husband?"

Naturally, some visitors left Lyuda's sessions feeling dissatisfied, even frustrated.

***

An intriguing event occurred in the life of an acquaintance of mine. A few years ago, shortly after I moved to Canada, I had a premonition that her husband would die in an accident. I didn't know precisely when or how only that it would be connected to his drinking problem. However, when I spoke with her, I lacked the courage to tell her directly about the impending danger, especially since she was already overwhelmed with despair over his alcoholism.

Years passed, and her husband was still alive and, as expected, still drinking. One day, I had the chance to meet her again, and we found ourselves together at Lyuda's home. As we talked, I mentioned in passing that not all predictions come true, and I expressed my relief that the grim premonition about her husband's death had not materialized.

The woman was surprised. "How could you stay silent about something so serious, about a threat to my husband's life?" she asked. Then she revealed something I hadn't known: besides Lyuda and me, another clairvoyant woman had also predicted her husband's untimely death. Yet none of the predictions had come true.

"Could all three of you have been wrong?" she asked. It seemed unlikely that three different people from three different parts of the world could see the same outcome and all be mistaken. So, what happened?

When she first heard the warnings from Lyuda and the other clairvoyant, she felt deeply conflicted. Each time her husband came home drunk, she was filled with resentment and pain, almost ready to accept his death to end her suffering. But her love for the father of her children, along with her conscience, ultimately prevailed. She would spend hours praying, begging God to forgive him. In her prayers, she forced herself to forget the pain he caused her and focused instead on the good times they had shared.

Occasionally, her husband would abstain from alcohol for a while, and during those times, their family life blossomed, filling their home with joy and peace. Eventually, she gave birth to the child she had long hoped for, a blessing further strengthening her resolve.

Ultimately, her determination, love for her family, and devotion to her husband helped avert the tragedy that once seemed inevitable.

As the three of us, Lyuda, my acquaintance, and I sat together over coffee, we discussed predictions, reflecting on which had come true, which hadn't, and why. Lyuda and I agreed that people always have a choice. Neither of us believed in fatalism. People bring fatalism into their lives by believing in pessimistic predictions. Once they accept them, every step pulls them closer to that outcome. Our thoughts shape our reality, attracting events accordingly. This realization empowers us to make conscious, positive choices that shape our lives.

Often, people act out of defiance, whether against "fate," others, or even themselves. "Everyone told me to do it one way, but I'll do it my way no matter what!" In the end, we always have choices. Even in seemingly hopeless situations, there is always a way out. And if the solution isn't immediately apparent, sometimes it's best to give things time. This emphasis on patience and hopefulness can make the audience feel more at ease and less rushed in decision-making.

Friends often say, "I've done everything I could, but the problem hasn't been solved, or it's only gotten worse." In those moments, I advise them to step back and leave the problem alone. Ask God or the Universe for help and stop worrying about it. This reinforcement of seeking help from a higher power can make the audience feel supported and less alone in their struggles.

I remember my grandmother's words: "If God gives the day, He will also give the bread." There's also a wonderful proverb: "The morning is wiser than the evening." So, when you go to bed, release your worries. Close your eyes, smile, and say: "God (or Universe), I've done everything possible. Now, I ask for your help and guidance."

Think of something pleasant or let yourself drift off to sleep. In the morning, you'll feel lighter, with a clearer mind. Within days or even hours, you may find that the problem has resolved itself in your favor.

An Angel's smile is a beautiful thing. And when you smile, the Angel, the Divine, and the Universe smile back at you.

My life has been filled with encounters with fascinating people. Once, someone asked me, surprised, why I seemed to have avoided crossing paths with dishonest or malicious individuals. First and foremost, the answer lies in the Law of Attraction: I attract kind, intelligent, and empathetic people because I strive to remain faithful to my moral principles. In other words, I consciously try to be kind, compassionate, and wise in my interactions. The known proverb "You reap what you sow" perfectly reflects this core principle: if you sow kindness, you will reap kindness.

Secondly, even when I encounter less-than-honest or well-intentioned people, the protection and guidance of my Angel and the Divine ensure that these encounters are brief and free from dramatic consequences. This connection brings me a profound sense of peace and reassurance. Whenever I feel uncertain about whether I can trust someone, I turn to them for guidance. Of course, I am not immune to mistakes, but I immediately ask for help when I feel uneasy.

Never hesitate to seek advice or assistance, especially when facing an important decision and feeling inner conflict or doubt.

There is a simple and accessible method for communicating with the Universe. It doesn't require any special skills or conditions. Begin by standing upright or sitting comfortably in a chair. Close your eyes and take a few seconds to relax. (As you become more attuned to receiving clear answers, you can communicate in any position and under any circumstances.) Formulate your question so that the answer can be "Yes" or "No." Then, focus on your breathing or the sensations in your body, allowing your mind to stay quiet and free from other thoughts, questions, or preconceived answers.

You may begin to feel subtle movements, slight tilts of your head, or shifts in your torso, like gentle vibrations or swaying. If your head naturally tilts forward, the answer is "Yes." If your head or body leans backward, the answer is "No."

This method is straightforward and requires no special preparation or conditions. In essence, it is a form of meditation. Many people associate meditation with yoga mats, isolated rooms, lotus positions, soothing music, or specific yoga practices. However, none of that is necessary. You can communicate with the Universe anywhere, anytime, and in any posture. The key is to feel physically comfortable.

If your clothing feels restrictive, loosen it or remove any tight belts. Relax your muscles by imagining waves of warmth or light starting at the top of your head and flowing slowly to the tips of your fingers and toes. Feel free to use these elements whenever possible if you find comfort in a dimly lit room, solitude, candlelight, or soft music.

The more natural and relaxed you are, the sooner you will learn to receive answers from the Universe.

I've heard from some devout believers and clergy that communicating with "spirits" is considered the work of the devil. Interestingly, the Bible is filled with stories of people communicating with God, as well as with seers and prophets. If someone sees an angel or the image of a saint, it is usually perceived positively, often generating excitement. However, when a person claims to communicate with angels, spirits, or God without being a devoted follower of a particular religion, they are often accused of fraud and labeled a sorcerer, witch, or even a follower of Satan.

Because of this, I have asked my Angel several times whether my communication with Him could be considered "unlawful" from the perspective of religion, society, or even common sense.

The Angel's answer has always been the same. People, without exception, see what they choose to visit in the world, interpreting everything through the lens of their own 'self.' This means that our perceptions and beliefs shape our reality. If someone believes in the existence of evil forces, such as the devil, demons, or wicked spirits, and lives in constant fear of encountering them, that fear attracts powerful streams of negative energy. They create the very images of these 'unclean spirits through their imagination.'

However, if one places their unwavering faith in the omnipotence of the Divine and embraces His universal love and protection, then there will be no room for the devil or evil forces in their life. This belief can inspire hope and bring a sense of peace and security.

We celebrated New Year's Eve at a relative's house one year. One of the relatives is a devout believer, but her faith is more blind than mindful; she doesn't realize that God is within her, that He watches over her, and that her life should be filled with joy and happiness because of her faith. Instead, her life is burdened with endless complications and troubles.

The problem is that she is always expecting something terrible to happen. She lives in fear of people, situations, and the unknown. She tries to adjust to circumstances instead of facing them and carries guilt and anxiety without any real cause.

Just a few minutes before midnight, she suddenly began lamenting about what she described as a near tragedy at church. According to her, the devil had misled her, causing her to leave behind a book, a bag, and some clothing after the service, and she was convinced that someone must have stolen them. The whole family tried to calm her down, explaining that the devil had nothing to do with it; she had forgotten the items, as she was naturally absent-minded and prone to forgetfulness. After all, we all leave things behind sometimes for no reason. The 'near-tragedy' was a simple case of forgetfulness but a sign of the devil's interference with her.

We reassured her that her belongings would likely be found and suggested she ask the priest or parishioners at the church about them. But instead of enjoying the joy of the New Year, she remained consumed by thoughts that the devil had interfered in her life, causing the mishap. She insisted that this was the devil's doing (though how could the devil possibly interfere during a church service?), and she feared it was a sign that the coming year would be filled with bad luck and misfortune — a "black streak" ahead. Her constant worrying ruined everyone's festive mood, and the chime of midnight passed by almost unnoticed.

Unfortunately, people often fail to realize how much they complicate their lives—and those around them- by creating artificial barriers to feeling the love, joy, and protection of the Divine.

***

Communication with the Universe, the Bioenergetic Information Field, God, spirits, angels, or any other form that feels meaningful to you can occur in many ways. As I mentioned, it is essential to remain open to receiving information at any time and in any form. Answers don't always arrive instantly, so patience is often required. Resistance, which can manifest as doubt, fear, or disbelief, must be fully released - allow the answer to come when you are ready to receive it.

The response to your question can come in countless forms. For example, you might "accidentally" turn on the TV or radio, and a specific phrase catches your attention; that is your answer. Or you may open a book, and the message you need will be waiting for you on the right page, and you'll instinctively recognize it as your answer. You could be riding the subway, and your eyes might land on a sentence from a magazine being read by a nearby passenger. A friend might unexpectedly call and say precisely what you need to hear, providing the clarity you seek. Even a passing stranger might say something in conversation that gives you the insight you were waiting for.

In my own life, I've encountered countless examples of receiving answers through different forms and channels. Every one of us is intricately connected not only to each other but also to other realms.

Whether we acknowledge it or not, this connection is a fundamental part of our existence. It has always existed and will continue, independent of our awareness or acceptance.

Not long ago, one of my husband's relatives passed away. He had been seriously ill, so in some ways, we were prepared for his passing.

One early morning, I dreamed: I saw a snow-covered forest, a lake with a river, and a beautiful white ship. We were bidding farewell to people setting off on an unknown journey into the vast whiteness. My husband was by my side, anxious about whether all the passengers had arrived on the ship in time. I felt a strange mix of calm and sadness when I woke up. I remembered something my father once told me: hours before his death, he dreamed of a white ship. His words were, "I saw a white ship. It's waiting to take me to another world."

That same day, my husband came home during his lunch break and, without saying a word, began lighting every candle in the house. I usually light candles, especially in the evenings, but we rarely light them during the day. Curious, I asked him what it meant, but he couldn't explain it clearly.

An hour later, we received a phone call informing us that my husband's relative, someone who had been like a father to him, had passed away. My

176

husband, Yuri, said quietly, "We are all connected. I lit the candles to burn away the negative energy and help my uncle pass peacefully, without resistance." In many spiritual traditions, lighting candles symbolizes hope, guidance, and the presence of the divine. By lighting the candles, Yuri invoked these spiritual elements to aid in his uncle's peaceful transition.

The soft light and flickering flames of the candles not only dissolved the accumulated suffering and pain from our relative's illness but also illuminated the path of his soul as it transitioned to the other world. Though we were separated by thousands of kilometers, in those moments, we were united, connected within the same energetic field as one whole.

If you remember that you are part of a unified whole, inherently connected to the Source, this connection will become more known each day, and through guidance, support, protection, and love, you will feel stronger within you.

***

Among the people we meet and turn to for help, some exploit our vulnerabilities, moments of despair, or the complexity of our problems. Unfortunately, many so-called "healers" operate under various titles, some even adopting seemingly "scientific" labels, but not all are honest with their clients. These individuals are often little more than frauds, skilled in extracting large sums of money for their supposedly supernatural healing services. They have a sharp understanding of human psychology, particularly the psychology of those in distress, people who are vulnerable and in desperate need of help.

How can we protect ourselves from being influenced by such individuals? By exercising critical thinking and being aware of the signs of manipulation, we can empower ourselves and take control of our decisions.

During times of stress and profound challenges, many people lose the ability to think clearly or analyze what they see and hear. On the one hand, they openly share their problems, seeking relief. On the other hand, they become so consumed by their troubles that they disconnect from reality and the people around them, often those who could offer better help than any so-called "specialist." Desperate, they may resort to extreme measures when they become most vulnerable to deceit.

Remember that transparency is key if you are unsure whether you can trust a healer or doctor. Ask direct questions about their methods, experience, and qualifications. Clear answers will reassure you that you seek genuine help and boost your confidence in your choices.

A rather interesting event occurred in my life. One day, a colleague of mine, a neurologist with whom I often discussed topics related to "psychic energy"— suggested that I attend courses led by a well-known doctor and master hypnotist, Dr. V. M. Kandyba. Dr. Kandyba has developed unique programs in autogenic training, a form of self-hypnosis that promotes relaxation and reduces stress. His teachings were quite progressive, which made them challenging for some conservative doctors to accept. His self-improvement and psychological auto-training programs were practical, effective, and easy to apply. To enroll, I needed to contact a representative at the city hospital.

I entered the crowded hallway of the city clinic, approached the office door, and knocked. Unfortunately, the door was closed. After waiting about fifteen minutes, I decided to leave. As I approached the stairwell, I encountered an elderly man. I walked past him, but unexpectedly, he called out:

"Excuse me, can I help you with something?"

His question surprised me, as I didn't appear to be a patient needing assistance.

"Perhaps, if you are Vyacheslav Anatolyevich," I replied.

And that's how we met. Vyacheslav Anatolyevich worked as a lawyer at one of the city hospitals, but, as I later learned, he was also involved in healing. He had been the local organizer for Dr. Kandyba's courses. However, Kandyba was ultimately unable to come and conduct the training.

From the beginning, Vyacheslav Anatolyevich treated me with kindness and deep respect. At one point, he asked me why I wasn't using my gift — the gift of healing. His question caught me off guard, as we hadn't discussed anything related to healing, and this was our first meeting.

After our conversation, he invited me to attend several of his healing sessions.

As I later discovered, Vyacheslav Anatolyevich referred to himself as a sorcerer. It was difficult to reconcile the image of an educated elderly man, a lawyer, and a sorcerer simultaneously. Whether this was entirely true or not, I learned that the League of Sorcerers of Ukraine at the time reportedly consisted of six practitioners of both white and black magic.

I have never supported magic, especially black magic, as people have distorted it over the centuries, burdened with countless rituals. It has lost much of its original moral intent to help others. The "profession" of a sorcerer or magician gained popularity after televised broadcasts in the Soviet Union showcased psychics supposedly charging water with energy and healing people through television screens. Even if some of these prominent "sorcerers" were genuinely transmitting unique forms of energy, whether psychic or biological, over long distances, these sessions often relied on elements of mass hypnosis, which I found troubling. My beliefs about magic and sorcery, shaped by my understanding of their historical and cultural contexts, influenced my interactions with Vyacheslav Anatolyevich and my decisions about our relationship.

Vyacheslav Anatolyevich generously shared several works by Dr. Kandyba and writings from other psychologists and parapsychologists. I found studying these materials highly enjoyable, though I didn't always agree with their conclusions. However, exploring another person's perspective on issues is always valuable and can help us become more open-minded and receptive to new ideas.

Reflecting on our first meeting, I recall an interesting moment. A warm spring thunderstorm raged outside while I was in Vyacheslav Anatolyevich's office. I kept looking out the window, hoping the rain would stop when I left the clinic. And that's precisely what happened. As Vyacheslav Anatolyevich walked me to the door, he casually remarked that the storm's end was one of his "magical tricks." I couldn't help but laugh, replying that perhaps it wasn't his doing but mine - after all, I had also wished for the rain to stop and for the sun to shine.

On several occasions, I asked Vyacheslav Anatolyevich why he chose to practice magic while also using Christian rituals. To me, magic and sorcery contradicted traditional Christian teachings, especially black magic — some fortune-tellers I had encountered openly admitted to using negative energy from black magic in some instances. However, Vyacheslav Anatolyevich's answer to my question was vague and elusive.

Despite our engaging conversations, I never became his student or follower. After I moved to Canada, I received a letter from him informing me that he had abandoned sorcery and relocated to Russia permanently. His decision earned my deep respect. I chose not to become his student or follower because I was wary of such a relationship's potential risks and ethical implications, especially given the controversial nature of his practices.

It's common these days to see large advertisements in newspapers and magazines promoting "famous hereditary fortune-tellers," promising, for a fee, to predict the future, bring back lost love, or cure every ailment. Often, the glowing reviews accompanying these ads are written by the self-proclaimed "clairvoyants" themselves. In modern times, this field has become a lucrative commercial enterprise.

One day, quite unintentionally, I was at a significant entertainment event, a party attended by numerous businesspeople and owners of various Canadian companies. My seat at the festive table was next to that of a "famous hereditary fortune-teller," whose advertisements were everywhere - in every local publication and on television. What immediately struck me was her brazen and vulgar behavior, her excessive fondness for alcohol, and her overly affected mannerisms.

Drunk on large quantities of vodka, she behaved provocatively, using foul language and profanity. The image of the kind, devout "hereditary fortune-teller," ready to help anyone in need, stood in stark contrast to the real woman I observed over three hours. Unfortunately, many people who seek help from such "hereditary" fortune-tellers, psychics, and healers encounter nothing more than a carefully crafted performance, one designed to evoke trust and empathy but motivated more by financial gain than any genuine desire to help. Be cautious when choosing where to seek help.

***

Healers can be categorized into several groups based on the sources they draw upon for their healing practices.

The first group comprises healers who act as intermediaries between individuals and the Source (God). These healers openly acknowledge their role as facilitators, empowering people to prepare to receive divine assistance independently. They assist in opening channels for healing energy, light, and love to flow, depending on the individual's openness. In this approach, the individual plays a passive-active role in the healing process, being passive in obtaining the energy and actively open to it.

The second group includes healers who have direct contact with the Source and channel healing energy from it. The person receiving healing remains entirely passive, regardless of their beliefs. Their primary focus is on the result, accepting help, irrespective of the methods involved. These healers often incorporate rituals, ceremonies, or objects into their practice, connecting to the Source to access specific types of healing energy.

The third group consists of healers who initiate the individual's contact with the Source but then step aside, allowing the person to take an active role in their self-healing. These healers open the door to a realm where the individual can explore and choose their path to healing. They teach people how to access that "door" whenever they need assistance, following the principle of "heal yourself." This approach emphasizes the individual's active role in their healing journey.

The fourth group focuses on group healing, harnessing the power of collective energy to amplify the healing effect. Research has shown that group prayers, for example, can positively impact the course of illnesses, promote recovery, and improve overall well-being, even when participants are geographically distant from one another. When similar energies align, they create resonance, significantly enhancing the effectiveness of the healing process.

While group healing can be beneficial, it's important to note that it may not suit everyone. For instance, some individuals may not feel comfortable sharing their healing journey with a group, or they may not resonate with the collective energy. Therefore, it's crucial to consider individual preferences and needs when choosing a healing method.

I asked my Angel for the most straightforward, quickest, and most reliable way to determine whether a healer is truly capable of helping restore health or improve a situation or if they are merely exploiting someone's vulnerability for personal gain.

In this context, the Angel serves as a guide, providing insights and guidance to help individuals make informed decisions about their healing journey.

***

Twilight is when day's light gracefully yields to night's darkness. The body is not yet ready for sleep, but a gentle fatigue settles over it, slowly wrapping itself around every part of you.

I sat in the garden beneath an ancient, towering tree, savoring the deepening stillness of the approaching night. The Angel sat beside me on the grass.

"I can't believe how much interest has grown in the things we've been discussing for years and what I've been writing about in my book," I said. "Fifteen or twenty years ago, all of this would have been dismissed as nonsense, and I couldn't even share these ideas with my family or close friends. Now, well-known figures speak about them in magazines, books, and television. Quantum physicists and religious leaders are exploring the same topics, and the old conflict between science and religion seems to give way to a shared direction. How do you explain this change?"

"Everything evolves," the Angel replied, his words carrying the weight of centuries of wisdom. "As one worldview fades, a new one takes its place. Humanity, along with every field of its activity, is entering a new era of development. A key feature of this era will be a deepening connection between people and Us, a conscious understanding of the processes unfolding in the Universe, the development of spiritual qualities, and the manifestation of Love."

"Some people predicted an apocalypse or catastrophic events in 2012," I said. "What do you make of that?"

"There are indeed massive shifts and realignments of energy taking place in the Universe, and these changes can manifest on the earthly level as well," the Angel answered. "But it is misguided to jump to conclusions, predicting the world's end or other catastrophic events shortly."

"Why?" I asked. "The people making these claims say they receive their information from Above. On top of that, many of them present scientific evidence from geological, tectonic, and meteorological research to support their warnings. How reliable are these statements?"

"The information people receive from Us is often misinterpreted and shared inaccurately," the Angel replied. "The shifting of energy flows within the Universe's development and existence is a constant phenomenon. But this doesn't mean these shifts are intended to destroy humanity. Humanity is destroying itself by constantly interfering with the natural laws of the Universe, which exist independently of human awareness or desires. Failing to understand these laws leads to unfortunate outcomes."

"Are you referring to climate change?" I asked.

The Angel smiled and continued, "Climate has undergone drastic changes long before humanity existed, shifting between heat and cold and back again. Earthquakes, volcanic eruptions, and floods were far more frequent and intense in the distant past than they have been in the last few tens of thousands of years, a span that, for the Universe, is nothing more than the blink of an eye. This is not where humanity's attention should be focused."

"Then what should we focus on?" I asked, intrigued.

"On the fact that humanity is destroying the conditions necessary for its survival," the Angel replied. "Imagine a room shared by several people. Some of them, without concern for others, begin littering, dumping waste, and defecating wherever they please. Eventually, the room becomes unlivable, and the residents start suffering from diseases. This is precisely what humanity is doing to the Earth. Irresponsible use of resources, especially energy, and careless environmental practices have set humanity on a path toward self-destruction."

For a few moments, I sat in silence, absorbing the Angel's words. They rang true, echoing the concerns many have been raising urgently.

"Tell me," I asked, "isn't that why we're feeling a stronger influence and more 'intervention' from Above?"

"Let's put it this way," the Angel replied, his patience a soothing balm. "People are turning toward us; more precisely, they are slowly returning to their roots. As they do, the interaction between us and humanity is becoming deeper, more meaningful, and more effective."

"So, it's like the old Chinese proverb: 'The teacher appears when the student is ready.'"

"Exactly. More and more people are reaching out to Us (and Our names may differ for everyone), not just for help, because a true student doesn't seek help but for knowledge."

"Now, back to the 2012 apocalypse," I said with a smile. "Will it happen or not?"

The Angel chuckled.

"That's just human curiosity," he said. "For everyone, the day of their death can feel like an apocalypse, the end of the world, at least for them. It marks the end of earthly light and, with it, earthly life. For some, it could even mean the end of suffering and liberation from a burdensome life. Is that such a terrible thing?"

"No, of course not, especially if life was filled with hardship," I agreed. "But many people are still afraid of these kinds of predictions."

"Then why not recall that extraordinary story from your life," the Angel suggested. "The one where you found yourself at the very heart of the Catholic Church on what was supposed to be the Day of the End of the World."

"And how can I save the world from ending?" I laughed. "Alright, let's revisit that story."

***

Italy... 09.09.1999, 9:09 a.m. Rome time.

It was a hot, dry, dusty Indian summer in the Vatican. Two women stood before St. Peter's Basilica, one in a wheelchair and the other on her own feet, eyeing the daunting staircase ahead.

"So many steps..."

"You go on without me. Leave me here. We'll not manage all those stairs with the wheelchair."

"No chance! We'll find another way, a roundabout path. Hold tight, and let's hope the ride isn't too bumpy."

Inside the vast, dimly lit space, the two women seemed like tiny insects beneath the towering arches. Michelangelo had once stood here, creating his masterpiece in the Sistine Chapel. It was a sacred place, a realm of awe and wonder. Camera flashes constantly flickered, disrupting the stillness and making it difficult to fully absorb the sense of holiness, but you adjusted over time. The quiet was only interrupted by the occasional cough or a whisper in an unfamiliar language, sometimes one you could recognize.

"How did we end up here today, of all days, when so many predict the end of the world?"

"Precisely because it's the end. Think of us as the saviors of the world."

"You're such a joker. I bet you'll go out with a smile or a joke as your last breath," I teased.

"Why the sudden talk about death? Go on, take a spin around the altar. Just try not to turn it into a race. We all know what your wheelchair can do," I teased. "I'll stay here and admire the art."

"All right, I'm off... Wait! Look behind you, turn around! That's your shadow... only carved in stone!"

Behind me stood an immense stone sculpture of a young, beautiful woman, around thirty years old. Her hair was neatly arranged, adorned with a modest crown. She held a massive stone cross in her right hand, supporting it so it wouldn't topple onto the visitors below. Her left hand was raised slightly as if offering a gentle greeting. At her feet, a stone plaque read:

SANCTA HELENA AVGVSTA

"Hey, snap out of it... Hello there! So, we finally meet."

"Helena? In St. Peter's Basilica? In the heart of the New Roman Empire?"

"And what's so strange about that? Why not?"

"Why not Mary? After all, she gave birth to God's son. Or at least one of the apostles? No, you shouldn't be here, especially not next to the altar."

"My dear, only God knows where I belong. When you get home, read; you might uncover even more surprising things."

"Still... you've truly surprised me. Is it easy carrying that cross?"

"Am I carrying it? Not really, just keeping it in place. The cross has always stood beside me, and I look like I'm resting... on my thorny path. See? I smile at everyone. People usually look at me, pray, and ask for protection. But you're the first to smile at me without asking for anything."

"I was going to ask something - for my friend. Will she be able to walk again?"

"She doesn't believe in me. She believes in God, but her faith is more in Fatima in Portugal. Fatima appears there from time to time."

"And why don't you appear to people?"

"I'm content here. And now I've appeared to you. Every day, new people come, though there are some familiar faces too... like Paul."

"You mean the Pope?"

"Of course. Who else? And don't forget, you have a meeting with him, too. Remember?"

"Yes, I remember. I can't quite wrap my head around it. How did this happen? How am I standing here, in the Vatican, and how am I about to receive a blessing from the Pope in a few days? I'm not anyone special. I haven't done anything remarkable."

"Do you remember what the Bible says? The greatest gift from God is the ability to dream and desire. And now, your dream has come true. Just make sure you dress well for the occasion."

"You're quite the jokester... and in a holy place, no less."

"The holiest place of all is the human soul!"

"Miss... Miss, I'm afraid you need to leave this area."

"???"

"I'm sorry, but your shoulders are uncovered, and it's not permitted to stay here dressed like that. Next time, please wear something with long sleeves."

"I apologize. I didn't even think about it. Please forgive me, I'll leave right away..."

"There are free shawls available near the main entrance. You can pick one up there. Strange that no one gave you one."

"I came in through the side entrance with my friend. I'll go now. Again, I'm sorry."

"You know what? Stay. Don't leave," the guard in black said with a friendly smile. "If anyone asks, just tell them I gave you permission." With that, he grinned and disappeared into the crowd.

"Helena... Hey! I'm still here, even if I am made of stone."

"Thank you for looking out for me. You are something else."

"And you're no different, still believing in miracles. Take care."

The two women, one in a wheelchair and the other walking beside her, carefully descended the steep steps, not wanting to exit through the side entrance again. A gentleman appeared just in time, helping them safely down to the sun-baked stones, worn smooth by centuries of footsteps.

The end of the world didn't happen, after all.

***

"So, on September 9, 1999, at exactly nine minutes past nine in the morning, the end of the world, which so many people had predicted, didn't happen," the Angel said.

"And not because I was in St. Peter's Basilica," I added. "When it was 9:09 a.m. in Rome, it was already 10:09 a.m. in Ukraine, and still the middle of the night in Canada. But I'm sure someone, somewhere, died at exactly 9:09 that day, in their local time."

"Exactly."

"And when you think about it, according to the Chinese calendar, it wasn't even 1999. For all we know, the 'end of the world' might have happened five thousand years ago."

"There have been countless predictions of the end of the world throughout history," the Angel said. "But people must remember they always have a choice, whether to believe those predictions, change their lives, or help others."

For a moment, we sat in silence. Billions of stars sparkled in the black sky above us.

"We've circled back to the concept of fear," I said. "Talk of the end of the world often seems like a way to hide the fear of death. What do you think?"

"Fear is nothing more than life's experiences, wrapped in layers of negative thoughts," the Angel replied. "It's a learned response, not an innate one. Do newborns have fear? No, not until they encounter something negative, usually accompanied by physical pain. This understanding can enlighten us about the nature of fear."

"No, not until they encounter something negative, usually accompanied by physical pain," I answered.

The Angel continued, "If a mother keeps telling her child that strangers or the 'bogeyman' will come and steal them away, the child will soon develop a fear of people. It will become difficult for them to tell the difference between someone kind and a 'boogeyman,' even though they are naturally connected to Us. Over time, this connection will be overshadowed by the lessons the parent imposes."

"I remember the lullaby my mother used to sing to me," I said. "And later, I sang it to my children:

Hush-a-bye, hush-a-bye,
The little gray boogeyman nearby.
He'll whisper, "Bring Lena to me,"
But I'll grab a stick—wait and see!
Shoo, shoo, boogeyman, be on your way,
You've no place here, no games to play.
Go away now, don't you try,
Don't you dare disturb our lullaby?
With a smile and a wave, I'll send him off,
No tricks, no sneers, no eerie scoff.
Our dreams are safe; the night is still,
And peace will reign, as is our will.
So, hush-a-bye, hush-a-bye, drift away,
The boogeyman won't come today.
Sleep sound and sweet till morning's light,
For all is calm, and all is right.
"She sang it to me every day when I was little."

"So, in the end, your mother was programming you to believe that if you misbehaved, some sinister figure would come to take you away, harm you, or bite you and that this figure needed to be driven off with violence, with a stick or punishment," the Angel said. "Children are fed stories about evil spirits lurking under tables or angry ghosts hiding in closets. Slowly but surely, they become withdrawn adults and distant from the Source. It can take years, or even an entire lifetime, for them to reconnect with Us."

"But isn't fear something we inherit through our genes?" I asked. "For example, many animals instinctively fear fire, even without encountering it. Scientists say this reaction could be linked to innate reflexes; embedded information passed down through the experiences of earlier generations. Does that mean all fear is hereditary?"

"If you shout suddenly at an animal or a person, it might startle them," the Angel replied. "But that's not the same as persistent fear. Some instincts are inherited, like the instinct for self-preservation when encountering the unfamiliar. But human fears are often nothing more than negative thoughts imposed on them from childhood by society, family, or loved ones. These fears reflect inner instability and a lack of confidence."

"Most people live trapped between the pain of the past and the fear of the future," I said. "Eckhart Tolle wrote in one of his books: 'When you create a problem, you create pain.' In other words, any obstacle, often self-imposed, becomes a problem that eventually becomes a painful experience of failure."

"Humans don't know what the future holds, so why fear what they cannot foresee?" the Angel asked.

"The past is over; it's gone and will not return. So why continue to revisit the pain of something no longer exists?"

Unfortunately, many people fail to realize that all their thoughts, including negative ones, such as emotional pain and fear, reside within them and are created by them. To illustrate this concept, I conducted several experiments with participants during my lectures on the Program of Happiness, Success, and Health.

At the start of the lecture, I asked the audience: "Right now, at this very moment, as I begin to introduce the program, do you have any problems?"

They responded, "No, not right now. We don't have any problems because we are listening to you."

After thirty minutes of the lecture, I asked again: "At this moment, do you have any problems?"

They all answered unison: "No, we have none so far."

"Wonderful!" I said. "That means that for the past thirty minutes, you've lived without problems."

At the end of the lecture, I repeated the same question. Everyone unanimously agreed that no new problems had arisen during the hour and a half of the lecture, and even their old problems had not occurred.

"Isn't it amazing," I asked, "that for an hour and a half of your life, you experienced no problems?"

This happened because the participants, fully immersed in the lecture, stopped generating negative thoughts. They were focused, engaged in discussions, laughing, and connecting.

I posed one final question: "In a few hours, night will come, and you'll sleep for about six to eight hours. Do you think new problems will arise during that time?"

"No, unless someone falls ill," they answered.

"And even then, it might not be your problem; you would simply be involved in someone else's. If we exclude unforeseen events, do you have any problems while you sleep?"

"No!" they answered in chorus.

"So, why not wake up in the morning feeling joyful, knowing you lived without problems for eight hours?"

***

James Ray, an extraordinarily successful man who teaches the science of success using the laws of the universe, shared his life philosophy during a teleconference in February 2007. He explained that no matter what his challenges, and he's had many, he begins each day with two simple words: "Thank you."

Ray expresses his gratitude every morning for the gift of life and health. He underlines the profound connection between gratitude and love, asserting that starting the day with positive emotions is a powerful magnet for more positivity.

By contrast, irritability, anger, and hatred inevitably draw unpleasant events into one's life.

The lesson is clear: our thoughts shape our reality. Replacing negative thoughts with gratitude, even for the smallest moments, opens the door to more joy and ease in our lives.

Fear is a negative emotion, and it is essential to eliminate it. I often hear the phrase, "You need to fight your fears." But is that truly the right approach? According to the Angel, a person must initially take control of every word and thought, gradually shifting their mindset from negative to positive. Fighting implies destruction. Instead of battling fears, we should replace them with positive thoughts, emotions, and feelings. This means acknowledging fear, understanding its root cause, and then consciously focusing on the situation's positive aspects.

Words laden with negativity should be replaced with synonyms that carry less weight or are neutral. For instance, instead of saying, "I hate this!" one could say, "This does not align with my views or interests." Similarly, rather than expressing, "I can't live like this anymore!" it's more constructive to say, "I need to change and improve my life (because I want to!)." Other examples include replacing 'I'm so stressed' with 'I'm feeling a bit overwhelmed' and 'I'm so fat' with 'I'm working on my fitness '.

Self-improvement requires time and consistency. When individuals approach me with chronic illnesses or complex conditions, I always remind them that resolving their issues and achieving healing may take a significant amount of time. Health problems often accumulate over months or even years. Consequently, transitioning from one state of physical and emotional well-being to another demands patience, sometimes a great deal.

The same principle applies to overcoming fears; it cannot be accomplished in just a few minutes. It is a journey that requires dedication and cultivating a positive mindset.

***

Following the release of The Secret, especially after several participants appeared on the Oprah television show, the public's reaction to the Law of Attraction and the messages conveyed in the film were nothing short of explosive. While most viewers embraced the film positively, others directed sharp and negative criticism towards its creators.

When I first saw Esther Hicks on television, I thought to myself that I would love to meet her. Her story of connecting with non-physical beings known as Abraham resonated deeply with my experience of establishing a connection with my spiritual guide, whom I call the Angel. Though I had known her words (or rather, their words) for over fifteen years, I hadn't recorded them as Esther did, nor did I believe this connection would evolve into a meaningful relationship.

Like me, Esther feared being ridiculed and misunderstood, even by those closest to her. She had made a vow never to write or speak about this connection, a promise I had made to myself more than once. Because of this shared experience, I felt a profound kinship with her.

However, I was uncertain whether I could meet Esther, listen to her, and converse. Now a renowned figure, she was in high demand worldwide for conferences, lectures, and seminars. How about arranging a meeting with her?

An unexpected connection emerged thanks to my friend Kristina. Knowing her deep admiration for the books by Esther and Jerry Hicks, I set out to obtain signed copies from Esther "by any means necessary." I wrote a letter to Esther, and within a few days, I received a response stating that she would be delighted to sign the books I wanted to gift Kristina. Two weeks later, those books were in my hands, with Esther's wishes. Kristina received them even earlier, on Christmas, and her joy was immeasurable. "Oh, how would I love to meet Esther in person!" she exclaimed. "Consider it done," I replied. Why not?

A day or two later, I 'accidentally' discovered that Esther would be coming to Toronto in March 2007, coinciding with Kristina's birthday, to participate in the 'I Can Do It' conference. This conference, known for its focus on personal development and spiritual growth, was a perfect platform for individuals like me who were eager to learn from and connect with spiritual leaders. To my surprise, I also learned that Sylvia Browne and several other notable figures would be attending the same event.

Sylvia Browne? This felt like a gift from the Angel! I had read several of Sylvia's books and seen her on Montel Williams' television show numerous times.

A few years earlier, she had visited a nearby town to give a lecture, but I hadn't been able to attend.

While Sylvia is not a personal idol of mine, I disagree with many of her views and haven't read all her works; I am continually impressed by her resilience. She has overcome poverty, endured a tumultuous marriage to an alcoholic, and faced societal criticism regarding her psychic abilities, ultimately achieving a level of fame that many envy. I respect her for her openness and straightforwardness; she doesn't conform to others and isn't afraid of attacks from harsh critics, cynics, skeptics, the press, or television.

Though I didn't want to ask her questions about my future, I was eager to see Sylvia "in the flesh," to feel her energy and hear her voice in person. I had even planned to choose a time to visit her at home, where she holds sessions to connect with people. And then, suddenly, I discovered Sylvia was coming to Toronto! Alongside her there would be Esther Hicks, Doreen Virtue, and Marianne Williamson.

Finally, we arrived at the Metro Convention Centre in the heart of business Toronto, where significant conferences, conventions, and seminars are held. The air was charged with anticipation as several thousand people had gathered for Sylvia Browne's lecture, many eagerly anticipating the chance to ask these renowned psychic questions about the future or other topics of interest.

Sylvia is an elderly woman, wise, approachable, and straightforward to talk to. She delivered a compelling two-hour lecture on human relationships, mainly on family dynamics. Many of her statements might not resonate well with staunch opponents of divorce or spiritual leaders advocating for submission and humility. It was evident that speaking was difficult for Sylvia due to her age; as she mentioned, her hectic schedule leaves her little time to rest. Yet, she also dedicates her efforts to supporting emerging talents, helping them gain recognition. Her energy impressed me, and I left the event feeling thoroughly satisfied and inspired by her presentation.

Her remarks about angels particularly stood out to me. Sylvia insisted that angels do not have wings, a sentiment I also shared, having never seen angels with wings. However, one morning, as she headed to the kitchen for breakfast, she unexpectedly saw an angel with wings. Sylvia's surprise and revelation were palpable as she remarked, "Once again, I was reminded that you should never use the word 'never' or be rigid in your beliefs, as a surprise will inevitably come along to challenge many of your convictions."

When the question-and-answer session began, a crowd of women, and even men, rushed to the stage to line up and ask questions, primarily about the future. I sensed Sylvia wasn't fond of making predictions, so she tried to move through the questions as swiftly as possible. Many people have voiced strong objections, accusing Sylvia of fraud because her predictions didn't come true. However, she has consistently stated that forecasts cannot be 100% accurate for various reasons. As a human being, she is entitled to make mistakes. Perhaps because of this, she is not fond of making predictions. Her true priorities lie in teaching lessons about uplifting the spirit, self-healing, self-belief, and prayer, as she is a remarkable teacher, psychologist, lecturer, and spiritual guide.

***

Esther Hicks is an extraordinarily kind and approachable woman. There is no hint of madness or deceitfulness about her. Perhaps her husband, Jerry, is more practical in managing her business trips, publications, and other affairs. Esther quickly enters a trance state without losing consciousness or contact with the surrounding world, relaying information from Above with such precision, clarity, and coherence that it is impossible to critique her (or Their) words. Indeed, it is impossible! I was thrilled to find that her messages perfectly aligned with what had been conveyed to me, and I never doubted for a moment that the Source was One.

For those who harbor doubt and skepticism in their hearts (and I certainly did), understanding and accepting Abraham's teachings, as conveyed through Esther, and recognizing this woman, as usual, can be challenging. This is entirely understandable. However, it's important to remember that Abraham is a conditional name, not a specific character. Abraham is neither male nor female nor a combination of both; it transcends material concepts entirely. The same applies to the Angel.

Listening to Esther restored a sense of balance and peace within me, which many of us lack daily. Her hands moved gracefully through the air as she spoke about comparing spiritual concepts to material ones, likening our lives to drifting down a river with the current.

After hearing a brief message from Abraham, many attendees began to ask questions. The responses were nothing less than manifestations of the Wisdom of Life, whether relating to existence on Earth or within the Universe. There were no momentary pauses or contradictory statements; the answers were seamless additions to everything already expressed or written, flowing like a continuous stream.

After Esther's presentation, my friend had the excellent opportunity to receive an autograph from this gifted woman and even take a photo together as a keepsake. I watched with delight as Esther interacted with the happy Kristina, knowing that many joyful and engaging encounters awaited us in the future. This personal connection with Esther made us feel included and part of the journey.

Following the release of the film The Secret and several books on the subject, a wave of speculation and excitement surrounded the Law of Attraction. Influential figures like Bob Proctor and his like-minded colleagues, who have generously shared knowledge and essentially variations of self-hypnosis through numerous emails, publications, phone seminars, and television shows, have played a significant role in this movement. However, this movement has also led to commercialization and the emergence of astonishing profits. Network marketing and multi-level marketing strategies have been integrated into this phenomenon. Bob and his wife, Linda, are actively involved in this arena, having even established network companies.

In contrast, Esther and Jerry Hicks have tactfully chosen to distance themselves from this artificially generated frenzy. They continue to focus on their work without launching extensive advertising campaigns or seeking media attention, maintaining their unique approach in the field. This dedication to authenticity is something I deeply respect.

***

A picturesque green meadow adorned with wildflowers, a patch of bright blue sky, the scent of summer, and me. I often envision this meadow when I seek light and joy and want to relax and unwind. I was reminded of it in the final scene of the captivating film Orlando, based on the eponymous novella by Virginia Woolf. This film received numerous awards worldwide despite being an erotic fantasy that explores the journey of its main character (whose gender changes several times) through time, delving into both feminine and masculine principles, as well as the meaning of life. It was released in 1992. In the final scenes, a joyful angel floats in the sky, singing a song for Orlando and her daughter.

Today, I am not alone in this meadow - my Angel is with me. My heart feels light and joyful.

"Hello, dear. It's been a while since we last spoke," I said.

"You've been busy... and we have communicated. It's just that those interactions were brief," replied the Angel.

"What's new?" I asked. "Tell me."

"What's new is that I see a lot of Joy in you."

I smiled contentedly once more.

"Yes, there is much joy because many good things have happened, and I find joy in life itself," I replied. "Many people would envy me at this moment."

The Angel reclined on the grass to gaze at the blue sky with me.

"My friend told me that I've been promoted to angelic rank," I mentioned.

"Angels have no ranks or levels; humans invented those concepts. But if your friend enjoys thinking that way, let her," the Angel replied, her wisdom shining through. "However, I can confidently say that you are undergoing positive changes. You are growing."

"How much can one grow? Especially sideways!" I laughed. "But you're right; I have grown. I've learned to be grateful."

"Let's discuss that, the State of Gratitude. Many people lack this state. What do you feel in such a state?"

"First and foremost, joy. I am alive, have family, children, food, a home, health, and so much more. I also have new ideas, interests, a desire to create, and even time to pursue many of my plans. I'm happy I can help others in various ways, and their lives are improving too."

"You're right; joy and gratitude are inseparable," said the Angel. "If gratitude is expressed without a smile, a sense of joy, and merely out of politeness, it isn't true gratitude. There is not a shred of sincerity or soul in such feelings."

"But expressing gratitude isn't so simple or didn't seem to me before. It's challenging to wake up early in the morning after a long, exhausting day, feeling a headache and having an empty wallet, and still joyfully start the day by being grateful for what you have."

The Angel replied, her understanding of human struggles evident. "Why isn't it simple? Once again, this is something people impose on themselves. Caught up in their problems, they often fail to see the struggles of others. As a result, it seems to them that there's nothing to be grateful for. Gratitude is a state of Love, Forgiveness, Hope, Joy, and Faith—positive emotions and feelings far more beneficial than negative ones."

"Tell me, Angel, do you have emotions and feelings?" I asked.

"No."

"So, you don't experience pain, joy, or love?"

"We do not experience pain or joy but feel love. However, it's difficult for people to understand how we experience it, what love means to us, and how it expresses itself from a human perspective."

"It expresses itself based on the principle that 'God is Love,' as far as I understand," I said.

"Absolutely. But what do you expect from God in that case?" asked my companion.

"Hmm... Love and, accordingly, protection, I suppose," I replied.

"It's simpler than you think. Since God is everything around you and within you, and you are part of this Whole, His Love already exists within you. You can express His Love towards yourself and others and feel His Love for yourself and others, especially since other people can also express this love. In short, there's no need to seek or wait for Divine Love, as it already exists in each of you, just as it does in all of us," said the Angel reassuringly.

"It seems so simple. But why do people still go to church, pray, and ask for the Almighty's forgiveness, protection, and love?" I asked.

"Do not confuse faith, religion, and beliefs. Remember that many people are conditioned to act this way, fearing punishment from Above, because fear can be used to manipulate a person and control their life. Spirituality should not be conflated with faith. In general, the concept of spirituality is a human measure of the soul, a sort of oscilloscope that gauges the degree of expression of various levels of energy that dominate within a person."

"Does this mean that the fear of God is unfounded?"

"Does this imply that if God is Love, then fear of Love is justified?" asked the Angel. "Should a mother feel fear towards her child, whom she loves and who loves her in return? Should a child feel fear towards a mother who loves him and whom he loves? All fears of God are completely unfounded. God does not need the love of people. We don't need it..."

I had heard this sentiment before, and those words didn't resonate well. If God doesn't need our love, prayers, or pleas, do we matter to Him? Can we expect and rely on His help in such a case? There's a saying that goes, "Hope in God, but don't be idle yourself."

"If You don't need the love of people, does that mean You don't need our problems? Are people praying or asking for help in vain?" I asked.

"No, not in vain at all," the Angel replied. "Because if you ask, you will be heard. But you must ask without anger, despair, or hatred. Prayer is a form of purification if it is sincere, not merely a show, an automatic recitation, a ritual, or a game."

"And it's even better to start with gratitude, right?"

"Exactly. Gratitude acts as a bridge of trust between a person and Us."

The wind played with my hair, and the birds' songs filled the air with beautiful melodies. No one was in a hurry, enjoying the idyllic scene of life.

"And yet, tell me more about You. There's so much talk about the laws of the Universe, but what do they represent?" I asked the Angel.

"A law is a creation of humans; it's a description of the sequence of a process—a statement often lacking proof or explanation. In practice, many processes can be termed laws. For example, the birth of a human ends with their death. Before humanity existed, laws did not exist; however, this does not mean that chaos reigned in the world and everything developed randomly. It was humans who studied the world around them and found explanations for many processes and phenomena through the order they named laws. Laws pertain to matter, including living organisms."

"But aren't there laws at the level of energies, even those energies that are currently inaccessible to human study and understanding?"

"There are," the Angel replied. "But they hold no significance for us. We do not adhere to laws. We exist beyond Time and Space, where such laws can function."

"Well, matter can transform into energy and vice versa. But what lies beyond energy?"

"Beyond energy, and within it, just like matter, there exists an Idea."

"An Idea? Isn't that the same as Information?" I asked.

The Angel smiled and replied, "They are not the same. An Idea is a dynamic process; it embodies the impulse of creation and creativity. Conversely, Information is often a static element that can be part of an Idea."

"So, the processes occurring in the Universe and beyond are not merely streams of Information and energy that transform into matter, exchanged chaotically, even if it seems chaotic. This is an essential component: creative creation if I put it that way.

"Correct," the Angel responded. "Information can be just a drop in the infinite ocean of Ideas, but without information, the Idea would be incomplete, much like an ocean without currents, waves, and life."

"An Idea... So, God?"

"Yes, God. This Idea requires constant movement in its development. God does not need people as physical shells or plants and animals in physical forms. He needs life as the result of the creative development of Ideas, especially thinking, feeling, dreaming, loving, and creating individuals."

"Because our thoughts, emotions, feelings, and much more complement the Idea?"

"Not only do they complement it, but they also expand and enhance it. A person in a state of genuine love, expressing love toward others, opens themselves up. This includes being in a state of gratitude."

"But don't the commandments teach us to love? Love God, love your neighbor."

"No, the primary commandments begin with the understanding that God is God, and there is no need to invent anything new, nor are there other gods or idols. The second commandment teaches you not to idolize objects or anything else, equating them with God."

"In the New Testament, Jesus teaches His disciples that the two most important commandments are to love God and love people. So where does the assertion that we need to love God come from if you say our love is unnecessary?"

"It comes from the same premise that 'God is Love.' If you love everything He has created, including people, then you automatically love God Himself. That is the love God needs. Imagine a situation where you love someone solely for their physical appearance while completely indifferent to their thoughts, emotions, and feelings, essentially, their life. Do you think your love would matter to that person? Likewise, God does not need worship, reverence, idolization, fanaticism, or admiration from people if He is separated or detached from what He has created and if people do not express love for one another first and foremost. So love, and you will be loved! And be grateful for the ability to love what you have, what was, and what will be."

***

I had to welcome the New Year 2008 without my family. My children and husband traveled to Ukraine to celebrate, while I voluntarily stayed in Canada with my beloved husky, Nanook. It was an excellent opportunity to take a break from household chores and work on several articles and essays. My Canadian friend Kristina decided to come over on New Year's Eve to ring in 2008 with me.

My relationship with Kristina extends beyond mere business; it's a friendship between two women with many shared interests. We often visit a café-bar in the heart of Etobicoke (a suburb of Toronto), where the staff knows us well. A cozy, quiet corner by the fireplace features two large, comfortable armchairs, an antique clock whose hands oddly move in the opposite direction, and a small table. It's a nook that feels like home. In this secluded, dimly lit space, we discuss various topics and share secrets, thoughts, and ideas while enjoying a glass of delicious white wine. These moments are our holidays for the soul, where no one interrupts us, and the hustle and bustle of daily life fades into the darkness of the night, allowing us to forget everything negative and talk freely about anything. Kristina loves esotericism and reads extensively on psychology, parapsychology, self-improvement, and communication with other worlds. While I don't share all her views, I respect her perspective and don't try to convince her that her opinions may be incorrect.

On New Year's Eve, Kristina brought a bottle of champagne and a divination wand. She wanted to connect with spirits or energies so we could ask them important questions and receive answers. To me, such "experiments" felt more like a game than something serious, primarily because I had taught Kristina more straightforward ways to communicate with them, and I didn't need intermediaries to get answers to my questions. However, I agreed to avoid disappointing my friend for bringing the wand.

We sat in the kitchen for two hours before the New Year. The aroma of delicious food filled the house, with a duck stuffed with apples roasting in the oven and champagne chilling in the refrigerator. Kristina prepared the wand and began the connection. She first told me that an intense, positive energy of feminine origin was contacting us. I didn't want to admit it was me, not some spirit. Then she said it was an Angel. I couldn't help but laugh. Wasn't she the one who had called me an angel before? She didn't understand what had amused me so much. At that moment, the Angel wasn't present; instead, he wasn't intervening. My friend began nudging me to ask questions, but what could I ask during such festive and joyful moments? This wasn't the time for questions; it was time for positive emotions. Kristina started asking questions herself.

However, listening to her answers only made me laugh more. It seemed I was playing with my energy and not allowing her to communicate with the "spirit" correctly. I then suggested, "Ask for the Angel's name." She began to recite the letters alphabetically, watching the wand's movement, and asked me to write everything down on paper. Since we were speaking in English, the name was recorded as CHOICE. At first, Kristina was taken aback: what a strange name for my spiritual guide! I understood everything briefly but kept a straight face, observing my friend's reaction. "What does 'Choice' mean?" she wondered aloud to herself and them. After all, we have a choice in naming! That was already my answer. It doesn't matter what we call them; those aren't their actual names but the names we assign to them; this was my explanation. The wand began to move, confirming I was right. Kristina always thought that otherworldly beings must have names, yet the choice of name was up to us. She didn't fully grasp the concept. I smiled at the Angel and said, "Thank you."

Now I know his name because I chose it, and that name is Angel. The name 'Angel' holds special significance for me, as it represents my positive energy and guidance.

***

As time flows, my life's events shift, bringing joy and challenges. Yet, with each passing day, I find increasing satisfaction in this journey, enriched by the wisdom I've gained. The most rewarding aspect for me is the opportunity to connect with fascinating individuals, each encountering a new chapter in the book of life.

My Angel's guidance has proven invaluable, leading me to gain more than I've lost. Have I truly lost anyone or anything? Everything in life is transient, coming and going as part of a more excellent plan. Whether joyful or bittersweet, each moment leaves a unique imprint on my life, making it a captivating and enjoyable journey.

I am not an angel but an ordinary person, though many imbue me with mystique and the supernatural. Every individual has something unique and original within them. In this context, the term "supernatural" does not apply, as we are all created from one Source, one Idea. This means that within each of us lies the essence of our Creator. You may call this Creator by different names - Nature, the Universe, God, Egregor, the Supreme Mind, the Information-Energy Field, Idea, etc. Does this change the fact that we are part of this unified Whole? We are unique particles, distinct from one another yet contributing to the uniqueness of this Whole.

Rejoice in Life! Rejoice in Love! If you find it difficult, look up at the blue sky, and you will see a joyful angel singing a song just for you.

List of Olena Berezovska's books

1. Мій шлях до істини. Березовська О.А. — 90 стор. Самовидав. Івано-Франківськ, Україна, 1986.

2. Интернет: Мифы и реальность заработка. Березовская Е.П. — 110 стр. Несколько онлайн-публикаций. Украина-Россия-Беларусь, 2000. (Ebook ISBN: 978-0-9867786-5-0)

3. Тысячиии... вопросов и ответов по гинекологии. Березовская Е.П. — 360 стр. Пресс-экспресс. Львов, Україна, 2008. (Print ISBN: 966-8360-08-7)

4. Ангел. Березовская Е.П. — 94 стр. Торонто, Канада, 2008. (Print ISBN: 978-1-997797-06-7, Ebook ISBN: 978-0-9867786-2-9)

5. День серебристого дождя. Березовская Е.П. — 107 стр. Торонто, Канада, 2008. (Ebook ISBN: 978-0-9867786-3-6)

6. Настольное пособие для беременных женщин. Березовская Е.П. — 400 стр. International Academy of Healthy Life. Канада-Украина, 2010. (Print ISBN: 978-0-9867786-1-2)

7. Подготовка к беременности. Березовская Е.П. — 200 стр. International Academy of Healthy Life. Канада-Украина, 2011. (Print ISBN: 978-0-9867786-0-5)

8. Гормонотерапия в акушерстве и гинекологии: иллюзии и реальность. Березовская Е.П. — 600 стр. International Academy of Healthy Life. Канада, 2013. (Ebook ISBN: 978-0-9867786-6-7)

9. 9 месяцев счастья. Настольное пособие для беременных женщин. Березовская Е.П. — 596 стр. ЭКСМО. Москва, Россия, 2015. (Print and Ebook ISBN: 978-5-699-80102-2)

10. Настільний посібник для вагітних. Березовська О.П. — 400 стор. Электронна версія. International Academy of Healthy Life. Торонто, Канада, 2016. (Ebook ISBN: 978-0-9867786-1-2)

11. Підготовка до вагітності. Березовська О.П. — 205 стор. Электронна версія. International Academy of Healthy Life. Торонто, Канада, 2016. (Print ISBN: 978-0-9867786-0-5)

12. Посібник для вагітних. Березовська О.П. — 392 стор. Манускрипт. Львів, Україна, 2016. (Print ISBN: 978-966-2400-55-7)

13. 1000 вопросов и ответов по гинекологии. Березовская Е.П. — 432 стр. ЭКСМО. Москва, Россия, 2017. (Print and Ebook ISBN: 978-5-699-80101-5)

14. Дочки-матери: Все, о чем вам не рассказывала ваша мама и чему стоит научить свою дочь. Березовская Е.П. — 288 стр. ЭКСМО. Москва, Россия, 2018. (Print and Ebook ISBN: 978-5-04-090021-3)

15. 9 місяців щастя. Березовська О.П. — 576 стор. BookChef. Київ, Україна, 2018. (Print and Ebook ISBN: 978-617-7559-18-3)

16. 9 месяцев счастья (второе издание). Настольное пособие для беременных женщин. Березовская

Е.П. — 596 стр. ЭКСМО. Москва, Россия, 2019.
(Print and Ebook ISBN: 978-5-04-098981-2)

17. Это все гормоны! Березовская Е.П. — 410 стр.
ЭКСМО. Москва, Россия, 2019. (Print and Ebook
ISBN: 978-5-04-101870-2)

18. Малыш, ты скоро? Березовская Е.П. — 384 стр.
ЭКСМО. Москва, Россия, 2019. (Print and Ebook
ISBN: 978-5-04-103359-0)

19. Когда ты будешь готова. Березовская Е.П. — 348
стр. ЭКСМО. Москва, Россия, 2020. (Print and
Ebook ISBN: 978-5-04-116932-9)

20. Здравствуй, малыш. Березовская Е.П. — 320 стр.
ЭКСМО. Москва, Россия, 2021. (Print and Ebook
ISBN 978-5-04-121120-2)

21. Педіатрія: у 3-х т. Т. 3: підручник для студ.
вищих мед. навч. закладів IV рівня акред.
Катілов О., Варзарь А., Валіуліс А., Дмитрієв Д.,
та ін. — 656 стор. Нова Книга. Вінниця, Україна,
2022. (Print ISBN: 978-966-382-931-9)

22. 9 місяців щастя. Посібник для вагітних
(оновлене й доповнене видання). Березовська
О.П. — 624 стор. BookChef. Київ, Україна, 2023.
(Print and Ebook ISBN: 978-617-548-122-6)

23. Коли тобі 35+. Як завагітніти й народити
дитину. Березовська О.П. — 256 стор. BookChef.
Київ, Україна, 2023. (Print and Ebook ISBN: 978-
617-548-124-0)

24. Когда тебе 35+. Как забеременеть и родить
ребенка. Березовская Е.П. — 290 стр.

International Academy of Healthy Life. Торонто, Канада, 2024. (Ebook ISBN: 978-0-9867786-7-4)

25. Angel. Olena Berezovska. — 256 p. International Academy of Healthy Life. Toronto, Canada, 2024. (Ebook ISBN: 978-0-9867786-8-1)

26. Ангел. Березовська О.П. — 270 стор. International Academy of Healthy Life. Торонто, Канада, 2024. (Print ISBN 978-0-9867786-9-8, Ebook ISBN 978-1-997797-00-5)

27. Grandma Lena's Bedtime Stories. Olena Berezovska. — 154 p. International Academy of Healthy Life. Toronto, Canada, 2024. (Print ISBN: 978-1-0691603-0-0)

28. Привіт, малюк! Як пройти четвертий триместр без турбот і хвилювань. Березовська О.П. — 290 стор. International Academy of Healthy Life. Торонто, Канада, 2024. (Print ISBN: 978-1-0691603-3-1)

29. Growing Up Strong: A Guide to Girls' Health and Well-Being. Olena Berezovska. — 422 p. International Academy of Healthy Life. Toronto, Canada, 2025. (Print ISBN: 978-1-0691603-4-8, Ebook: 978-1-0694544-6-1)

30. Вечірні казочки бабусі Олени. Березовська О.П. — 180 стор. International Academy of Healthy Life. Toronto, Canada, 2025 (Print ISBN: 978-1-0691603-1-7)

31. Вечерние сказки бабушки Лены. Березовская Е.П. — 172 стр. International Academy of Healthy

Life. Toronto, Canada, 2025 (Ebook ISBN: 978-1-0691603-2-4).

32. The Curious Escapades of a Corpse Named Jack. Book 1. Olena Berezovska. — 148 p. International Academy of Healthy Life. Toronto, Canada, 2025 (Print ISBN: 978-1-0691603-5-5, Ebook IBSN: 978-1-997797-02-9)

33. Основи здоров'я дівчаток: Практичний путівник для батьків. Березовська О. — 570 стор. International Academy of Healthy Life. Toronto, Canada, 2025 (Print ISBN: 978-1-0691603-6-2, Ebook: 978-1-0694544-7-8)

34. The Curious Escapades of a Corpse Named Jack. Book 2. Olena Berezovska. — 112 p. International Academy of Healthy Life. Toronto, Canada, 2025 (Print ISBN: 978-1-0691603-7-9, Ebook ISBN: 978-1-997797-03-6)

35. Hormonal Intelligence: How Hormones Shape Health and Well-being. Olena Berezovska. — 478 p. International Academy of Healthy Life. Toronto, Canada, 2025 (Print ISBN: 978-1-0691603-8-6, Ebook IBSN: 978-1-0694544-4-7)

36. Все про гормони: Таємна мова вашого тіла. Олена Березовська. — 460 с. International Academy of Healthy Life. Торонто, Канада, 2025 (Print ISBN: 978-1-0691603-9-3, Ebook IBSN: 978-1-0694544-5-4)

37. Дивовижні пригоди трупа на ім'я Джек: Книга 1. Олена Березовська. — 180 с. International Academy of Healthy Life. Торонто, Канада, 2025

(Print ISBN: 978-1-0694544-0-9, Ebook IBSN: 978-1-997797-04-3)

38. Підготовка до вагітності: Посібник з усвідомленого батьківства. Олена Березовська. — 468 c. International Academy of Healthy Life. Торонто, Канада, 25 травня 2025 (Print ISBN: 978-1-0694544-41-6, Ebook IBSN: 978-1-0694544-8-5)

39. DIY Bestseller: How to Write, Publish, and Market Your Book in the AI Era. Olena Berezovska. — 432 p. International Academy of Healthy Life. Toronto, Canada, 2025. (Print ISBN: 978-1-0694544-2-3, Ebook IBSN: 978-1-997797-01-2)

40. Mind Over Muscle: A Journal for Teen Athletes. Olena Berezovska. — 56 p. International Academy of Healthy Life. Toronto, Canada, 2025. (Print ISBN: 978-1-0694544-3-0, Ebook IBSN: 978-1-0694544-3-0)

www.ingramcontent.com/pod-product-compliance
Lightning Source LLC
LaVergne TN
LVHW051401080426
835508LV00022B/2927